Alev Masarwa

Praising Damascus: City Panegyrics as a Literary Genre and a Concept of Urbanity

WWU
MÜNSTER

Wissenschaftliche Schriften der WWU Münster

Reihe XII

Band 35

Alev Masarwa

Praising Damascus: City Panegyrics as a Literary Genre and a Concept of Urbanity

Georg Olms Verlag
Hildesheim · Zürich · New York

Wissenschaftliche Schriften der WWU Münster
herausgegeben von der Universitäts- und Landesbibliothek Münster
http://www.ulb.uni-muenster.de

ulb Münster

Eine Publikation in Zusammenarbeit mit dem Georg Olms Verlag
https://www.olms.de

OLMS

Bibliografische Information der Deutschen Nationalbibliothek:
Die Deutsche Nationalbibliothek verzeichnet diese Publikation in der Deutschen Nationalbibliografie; detaillierte bibliografische Daten sind im Internet über https://www.dnb.de abrufbar.

Dieses Buch steht gleichzeitig in einer elektronischen Version über den Publikations- und Archivierungs-server der WWU Münster zur Verfügung.
https://www.ulb.uni-muenster.de/wissenschaftliche-schriften

Alev Masarwa
„Praising Damascus: City Panegyrics as a Literary Genre and a Concept of Urbanity“
Wissenschaftliche Schriften der WWU Münster, Reihe XII, Band 35
Georg Olms Verlag, Hildesheim

ISBN 978-3-487-16272-0 (Druckausgabe Georg Olms Verlag)
ISBN 978-3-8405-0276-7 (elektronische Version)
DOI 10.17879/32099577185 (elektronische Version)
URN urn:nbn:de:hbz:6-32099577467 (elektronische Version)

direkt zur Online-Version:

Satz: Alev Masarwa
Umschlag: ULB Münster

Contents

Acknowledgements

This study is an expanded version of a paper entitled "Urbane Tropen und tropische Urbanitäten" presented in 2013 at the 32nd German Conference of Oriental Studies in Münster. I would like to express my sincere gratitude to Geert Jan van Gelder, who readily shared with me some of his vast knowledge in Arabic literature and provided insightful comments and corrections on an earlier draft of this study. My wholehearted thanks also go to Ian Copestake, Ronald Mayer-Opificius, and Samir Mubayd for their encouraging and helpful comments and corrections.

I would like to thank the editors of the Wissenschaftliche Schriftenreihe der Westfälischen Wilhelms-Universität Münster for including this work in the series. I am indebted to the team "Servicepunkt Publizieren" of the Münster University and State Library for their professional assistance in editing, formatting, and providing feedback throughout the preparation of this publication.

Praising Damascus: City Panegyrics as a Literary Genre and a Concept of Urbanity

The vast corpus of city panegyrics in prose and poetry gives testimony to the dynamics of urban life and urban consciousness, as it has also always been a source of civic pride and belonging. The vigorous form of aesthetic elaboration about cities was both persistent and open for contestation at the same time. A striking example, which attests to this contestation and the dynamics of city praise is a city-slam (*mufāḫara / munāẓara*) between Baghdad and Damascus, written in ca. 16th century Syria.

Taking panegyric literature about Damascus as an example, this study discusses its literary elaboration and established motif traditions in relation to a wide range of textual representations of cities. Focussing on predominantly rhetorical elements and their inversion, rather than on topographical history the analysis will include other cities besides Damascus. Exposing the aesthetic devices and analyzing their functions by inverting them according to the rules of poetic speech offers a convenient tool for a more adequate understanding of city panegyrics, and the cultural perception of cities. It will be shown that panegyrics contain assertions relating both to praise and criticism.

The relevance of cities for Islam as a social and historical space is obvious: It is here, in cities, that community, ritual, ethics, education, power and law are realized.[1] The mainly orientalist notion of a stagnant Islamic society – as can also be found in the work of Max Weber, who stresses, for example, the absence of formal urban privileges, the lack of autonomy of cities and a generally hidden sense of civicness in the Asian city in contrast to its occidental counterpart – seems to restrict the application of

1 Carl Becker: *Islamstudien. Vom Werden und Wesen der islamischen Welt* (Leipzig: Meyer, 1924), 1: 55.

a concept of urbanity to 'Islamic' cities.[2] On the contrary, city related texts do not support the alleged nonparticipation of urbanites in a city's political events as it appears in culturalist discourse, i.e. the sharp division of the spheres of ruler and ruled in urban poetry.

However, a narrow understanding of 'urbanism' without considering urban consciousness and perception, as it is expressed particularly in textual sources, facilitates Islamic 'otherness'. The reluctance to exploit those sources is perhaps due to the fact that such 'soft' data is mostly given in *adab*-literature.[3] City-related texts, be they in Arabic or in western languages, were read according to the paradigm of factuality and asked whether they reflected and verified 'historical reality'. This method of perception, which reflected a more positivist stance, inevitably led to an understanding of city-panegyrics as almost hagiographical texts. Whereas for modern critics of such a positivistic approach, city panegyrics were customarily perceived as ornamental passages to the 'real' historical narrative. In actual fact, they were mostly ignored for transmitting a mere

---

2 Max Weber: *Wirtschaft und Gesellschaft: die Stadt* (Tübingen: Mohr (Paul Siebeck), 1922), 149–151, also 522–536; see also Wolfgang Schluchter (ed.): *Max Webers Sicht des Islams. Interpretation und Kritik* (Frankfurt a. M.: Suhrkamp, 1987); Hinnerk Bruhns and Wilfried Nippel (eds.): *Max Weber und die Stadt im Kulturvergleich* (Göttingen: Vandenhoeck und Ruprecht, 2000), esp. 10; Sami Zubaida: "Max Weber's The City and the Islamic City", in: *Max Weber Studies* 6 (2006), 111–118 and Stefan Peychev: "Max Weber and the Islamic City" [http://www.academia.edu/329856/Max_Weber_and_the_Islamic_City].

3 Li Guo: "Reading Adab in Historical Light: Factuality and Ambiguity in Ibn Dāniyāl's 'Occasional Verses' on Mamluk Society and Politics", in: *History and Historiography of Post-Mongol Central Asia and the Mongol East*, ed. Judith Pfeiffer and Sholeh A. Quinn (Wiesbaden, Harrassowitz, 2006), 400 and Martyn Smith: "Finding Meaning in the City: al-Maqrīzī's Use of Poetry in the Khiṭaṭ", in: *Mamluk Studies Review* 16 (2012), 143.

adulation and a rhetorical phantasm of the empirically real city[4] or for proving the existence of a mere paradigmatic epigonism of the epideictic rhetoric of the Greeks, unless some anti-authoritarian perspectives were offered, which were considered more trustworthy. In such cases, most of the former scepticism towards rhetorical devices and genre specifics was ignored.[5]

Between these approaches, the main features and elaborately encoded messages of literary texts are usually lost. In his study, Hartmut Kugler offers a convenient tool for dealing with city panegyrics and city descriptions as sources, namely by focusing on the perception of a city, of pat-

4 In his study of the descriptions of Cairo and Damascus in *1001 Nights*, Peter Bachmann points out that the city descriptions present more or less real and not imagined/magic cities, even when the narrative frame is fictional: "Im Unterschied zu solchen Zauber- oder Legendengeschichten werden Kairo und Damaskus als reale Orte genannt, vor allem wohl deshalb, um arabischen Hörern (Lesern) gegenüber als eine Art Beglaubigung des bunten Erzählens zu dienen. [...] Daß überhaupt Örtlichkeiten und Bewohner realer Städte – mehr oder weniger treu geschildert – in Tausendundeiner Nacht genannt werden, zeigt, daß viele der Geschichten dieser Sammlung keine Märchen im Sinne unserer Volksmärchen sind, die im Irgendwo spielen, sondern Sagen, Legenden, Abenteuergeschichten, Kriminalgeschichten, ortstypische Schwänke und Ähnliches." See his: "Kairo und Damaskus in Tausendundeiner Nacht", in: *Orte der Literatur*, ed. Werner Frick et al. (Göttingen: Wallstein Verlag 2003), 50–67, citation from 66, see also 67.

5 This antagonism is not restricted to the Arabic literary tradition. For a discussion of city panegyrics of medieval European cities, especially for Nuremberg, see the in-depth study by Carla Meyer: *Die Stadt als Thema* (Ostfildern: Jan Thorbecke Verlag, 2009), 245–251, esp. 248–249. See also fn 17 in this study.

terns of description and thought for which the author provides a draft, instead of contrasting (city-) imagery with (city-) reality.[6]

> *Einer Stadt, wie sie ist, stellt der Text eine Stadt, wie sie sein soll, gegenüber. So verstanden, ist ein Städtelob immer beschreibend und normierend. Es liefert nicht einfach Beschönigungen einer unzureichenden Stadtwirklichkeit, sondern es liefert einen Entwurf.*[7]

On the problem of cohesion of *topoi* and reality, Kugler points out that the academic approach to city-panegyrics, which was only focused on the rhetorical devices according to the antique rhetoric tradition ignored the progress and dynamics within this genre and within urban reality. The opposite side, a mere historical approach, is seen to cherry-pick only valuable data while neglecting the literary devices and the textual cohesion.[8]

The dependency of Arabic city-panegyrics on classical patterns for the genre was already recognized by Grunebaum and in parts also by Ewald Wagner.[9] However, and according to Kugler, one should also not be tempted to read these texts solely as a rhetorical descriptive pattern that does not reflect reality. Metropoleis like Damascus, Baghdad and Cairo

6 Hartmut Kugler: *Die Vorstellung der Stadt in der Literatur des Mittelalters* (München: Artemis und Winkler, 1986), 26.

7 Kugler: *Die Vorstellung der Stadt in der Literatur des Mittelalters*, 31.

8 Kugler: *Die Vorstellung der Stadt in der Literatur des Mittelalters*, 21–26.

9 For the Arabic tradition in general, see Gustave E. von Grunebaum: "Observations on City Panegyrics in Arabic Prose", in: *Journal of the American Oriental Society* 64 (1944), 61–65 and Ewald Wagner: *Die arabische Rangstreitdichtung und ihre Einordnung in die allgemeine Literaturgeschichte* (Wiesbaden: Steiner Verlag, 1963). On the emergence and tradition of poetic city panegyrics up to the end of ʿAbbasīd times, see Hussein Bayyud: *Die Stadt in der arabischen Poesie, bis 1258 n. Chr.* (Berlin: Schwarz Verlag, 1988).

are not just urban spaces where cultural forces work but are also objects of these forces' creativity. As a consequence of this, the incorporation is mutual. Depending on the genre and its conventional shapes, the topographical perception of space collides with a relativist aesthetic perception of space in poetry.[10] Sometimes, aš-Šām is stated and Damascus is meant while in other cases the term signifies the larger geographical area of *bilād aš-Šām*.[11] Sometimes, a quarter of Damascus or even one house is praised with the whole of *aš-Šām* profiting from this and even when the city is not named but merely implied, the praise for Damascus is apparent. It is also worth considering that the Damascus of a geographical text is not necessarily the same as the Damascus of a *qaṣīda* – i.e. the scope of objectifying urban space derives primarily from the formal demands of the 'genre' and of 'motif' formation.

---

10 Since abandoning a mere substantialist perception of time and space, proponents of the spatial turn (topographical turn) tend to dominate the discourse within cultural studies, where these key terms are occupied with relational and more action-based concepts. See Stephan Günzel: *Topologie. Zur Raumbeschreibung in den Kultur- und Medienwissenschaften* (Bielefeld: transkript, 2007), esp. 13–29.

11 Zayde Antrim: *Routes and Realms: The Power of Place in the Early Islamic World* (New York: Oxford University Press, 2012) for a substantial discussion of spatial paradigms and the motifs of belonging. See also Stefan Heidemann: "Entwicklung und Selbstverständnis mittelalterlicher Städte in der Islamischen Welt (7.–15. Jahrhundert)", in: *Was machte im Mittelalter zur Stadt? Selbstverständnis, Außersicht und Erscheinungsbilder mittelalterlicher Städte*, ed. Kurt-Ulrich Jaeschke and Christhard Schrenk (Heilbronn: Stadtarchiv Heilbronn, 2007), 203–244 and Torsten Wollina: "What is a City? Perceptions of Architectural and Social Order in 15th-Century Damascus", in: *ASK Working Paper*; 04 (Bonn: Annemarie Schimmel Kolleg – History and Society during the Mamluk Era (1250–1517), 2012).

It is due to the dominant role of literary arts (especially poetry) as immediate transmitters of discourses, that a city's rank, once labeled with a famous literary ascription (i.e. a special city branding), persistently prevails. Nevertheless, this ranking was always open for contestation, and evolved into the genre of literary debate (*mufāḫara / munāẓara*) between cities such as Mecca and Medina, Basra and Kufa, Cairo and Damascus and Baghdad and Damascus. An example of the latter pair (*mufāḫarat ad-Dimašqī wa-l-Baġdādī*) will be presented and analyzed in the last section of this study.

Organism

Since antiquity, metaphors of organism and body have permeated the discourse about urban environment: the city lives, falls sick, dies, grows, prospers and pulsates.[12] The city is anatomically organized and has a life of its own: it has a heart, lungs and arteries. Bearing human characteristics, the cities were also described within the ensemble of other cities, referring to a greater organism. Their social characteristics used to emphasize its honor and rank among other cities. Consequently the (human) characteristics of cities were also transferred upon the cities' inhabitants. Such comparisons are not foreign to Arab literary tradition. According to a very popular albeit weak tradition, '*the earth was created like a bird: Syria is the head, Egypt the tail and Iraq the wings*'[13]. There are also some

---

12 On the analogy of body/organism and cities in antiquity, see Felix Mundt: "Der Mensch, das Licht und die Stadt. Rhetorische Theorie und Praxis antiker und humanistischer Stadtbeschreibung", in: *Cityscaping. Constructing and Modelling Images of the City*, ed. by Therese Fuhrer, Felix Mundt, Jan Stenger, 179–206 (Berlin: De Gruyter, 2015), 192 and 197–198.

13 Ernst Gruber: *Verdienst und Rang. Die Faḍā'il als literarisches und gesellschaftliches Problem* (Freiburg i. Br.: Schwarz-Verlag, 1975), 75–76 with several variants of this tradition.

expressive traditions of transformation and distribution of cities/regions' characteristics upon the inhabitants as a divine providence. Pointing to the paired occurrences of human and civilizing attributes (as apparent binary opposites) in an unusual personification, the tradition leaves the toponyms neutral. The following example inverts cause and effect in a *metalepsis*:

> *Reportedly ʿUmar Ibn al-Ḫaṭṭāb asked Kaʿb about the lands and their situation. He said: "Prince of the Faithful! When God created all things, he joined each with another:*
>
> *The mind said: I will attach myself to ʿIrāq. Whereupon knowledge said: I will join you.*
>
> *Wealth said: I will attach myself to Syria. Whereupon sedition said: I will join you.*
>
> *Poverty said: I will attach myself to the Ḥiǧāz. Whereupon frugality said: I will join you.*
>
> *Severity said: I will attach myself to the Maġrib. Whereupon the bad charccter said: I will join you.*
>
> *Beauty said: I will attach myself to the East. Whereupon the good character said: I will join you.*
>
> *Misery said: I will attach myself to the desert. Whereupon health said: I will join you."*[14]

---

[14] Gruber: *Verdierst und Rang*, 79 f. with considerable variants of this account. One variant is related in the *Manāqib Baġdād* of Ibn al Ġawzī (d. 597/1201), once in favor and once to the disadvantage of Iraq (Abū l-Farāǧ Ibn al-Ǧawzī: *Manāqib Baġdād*, ed., Muḥammad Bahǧat al-Aṯarī (Baġdād: Maṭbaʻat Dār as-Salām, 1342/1923), 5–6.

The body metaphor is also employed in descriptions of Mecca and Medina, as two of the most important cities to Islam. Among their numerous epithets are: for Mecca *umm al-qurā* (mother of cities) and for Medina *ta'kulu l-qurā* (that, which devours cities).[15]

For Damascus religious tradition, geographers, poets and travelers bestowed her with the most honorable and eminent titles for her beauty and pride, such as *aš-Šam aš-šarīf* (the noble Šām); *ğannat al-arḍ* (Paradise on Earth); *Dimašq al-fayḥā'* (diffusive, for the idea of fragrance); *Dimašq: dār as-surūr* (for the idea of pleasure); *Dimašq: dār an-na'īm* (House of Bliss); *'arūs ad-dunyā* (Bride of the Earth); *sayyidat al-mudun* (Queen/ Mistress of Cities); *ġurrat ad-dunyā* (Blaze of Earth) *etc.* These nearly mandatory epithets display frequently employed images in all literary genres focusing on the city of aš-Šām. They marked Damascus and with it greater Syria and gave it a discursive rank, until denied for any good reason.

In particular, poetic elegies in the pattern of the *marṯiya* (lament) about cities use this corporal imagery: e.g. when Abū Tammām writes about the 'decline' of Baghdad, which the author likens to '*an old woman ... while a blossoming concubine* [Samarrā'], *bright as the sun, even more beautiful in the eye of her beholder, pushes to get next to her*'[16]. The western parallel would be the genres of the *ubi sunt* (in the specific case of fallen cities) and *laus urbis* (in the case of panegyrics).[17] In the laments about

15 Qur'ān 42:7 and *ḥadīṯs* cited in Gruber: *Verdienst und Rang*, 71.

16 Abū Tammām cited in Bayyud: *Die Stadt in der arabischen Poesie*, 118 (verse 4). See also Gustave E. von Grunebaum: "Aspects of Arabic urban literature, mostly in the ninth and tenth centuries", in: *Islamic Studies* 8 (1969), 281–300, here 284 and fn 19.

17 Many *laudes urbium* were written e.g., in Germany particularly during the age of humanism. Almost every larger German city became an object of a *laus urbis* (foremost Nuremberg); but also many Italian cities, as well as Paris, London,

existing or fallen cities, past virtues were nostalgically made present, e. g. the good old days. In particular, *vanitas* motifs engage with the fleeting nature and vicissitudes of life. In addition to criticism of the social order and the critique of domination, concepts of an ideal order emerge from praise (of cities) and invectives (against their destroyers).

The vast poetic corpus of *ritāʾ al-mudun* (laments for cities) and also *ḥanīn ilā l-awṭān* (longing for home/s) poems are another rich source for encountering aesthetics, urbanity, history, regional identity, political and military events, particularly in times of crisis. However, the genre of *ritāʾ al-mudun* deserves a separate discussion, which is beyond the scope of this study.[18]

Constantinople and even St Petersburg were objects of city panegyrics. See Eugen Giegler: *Das Genos der Laudes urbium im lateinischen Mittelalter. Beiträge zur Topik des Städtelobes in der Stadtschilderung* (Diss. Würzburg, 1953); Hartmut Kugler: *Die Vorstellung der Stadt in der Literatur des Mittelalters*; Jon E. Lendon: *Empire of Honour: The Art of Government in the Roman World* (Oxford: Clarendon Press, 1997); Carla Meyer: *Die Stadt als Thema. Nürnbergs Entdeckung in Texten um 1500*; Mundt: "Der Mensch, das Licht und die Stadt", 179–206; Andreas Rhoby: "Stadtlob und Stadtkritik in der byzantinischen Literatur", in: *Byzantinische Sprachkunst. Studien zur byzantinischen Literatur*, ed. Martin Hinterberger (Berlin: De Gruyter, 2007), 277–295 and Heide Weißhaar-Kiem: *Lobschriften und Beschreibungen ehemaliger Reichs- und Residenzstädte in Bayern bis 1800: Die Geschichte der Texte und ihre Bibliographie* (Mittenwald: Mäander, 1982).

18 There are substantial contributions on this genre with further references. See, for example, Charles Pellat: "Mart͟hiya", in: *Encyclopaedia of Islam*, 2nd ed., 6: 602–608; Geert J. van Gelder: "City panegyric, in Classical Arabic", in: *Encyclopaedia of Islam, Three* [online]; Alexander E. Elinson: *Looking Back at al-Andalus. The Poetics of Loss and Nostalgia in Medieval Arabic and Hebrew Literature* (Leiden: Brill, 2015); Cynthia Robinson: "'Ubi sunt': Memory and Nostalgia in Taifa Court Culture", in: *Muqarnas* 15 (1998), 20–31 and Ibrahim Sinjilawi: *The Lament for Fallen Cities. A Study of the Development of the Elegiac Genre in Classical Arabic Poetry* (Ph. D. Diss., University of Chicago,

City panegyrics in prose and poetry

Rhymed prose and poetry are the most popular forms of city panegyrics. Ibn Ǧubayr's (d. 540/1145) travel account offers perhaps the most impressive experience of the city of Damascus and for the genre of prose-texts the most generic. The *maḥāsin* (beauties, merits) of Damascus are all the more striking because the traveler was disappointed by the commonly praised beauties of Baghdad, which according to him was a city that was only a shadow of its former self. In this kind of enumeration of positive aspects of urban topics as markers of difference to other cities the author had in mind, we receive the information about what a 'good' city has to offer while considering the rules of rhymed prose (Arabic: *saǧʿ*). It is full of corporal metaphors integrating material prosperity, hyperboles of blessedness with the natural habitat dazzling the spectators' eyes with her beauty:

> *Damascus is the paradise of the east and the rising place of its radiant beauty. It was the last of the cities of Islam whose hospitality we enjoyed, and the bride of the towns we saw. We found it adorned with flowers of fragrant plants, displaying silk-brocaded garments in the form of gardens. The position it holds in the realm of the beauty is firmly established, sumptuously ornamented she sits on her bridal throne*[19].[20]

1983). On the 'fall of cities' see also Alev Masarwa: "Der Fall Alexandrias in den Städteklagen Ibn Abī Ḥaǧalahs und seiner Zeitgenossen", in: *The Sultan's Anthologist: Ibn Abī Ḥaǧala and His Works*, ed. Syrinx von Hees and Nefeli Papoutsakis (Baden-Baden: Ergon, 2017).

19 Damascus is approximately 800m above sea level.

20 Translated by Philip K. Hitti: *Capital Cities of Arab Islam* (Minneapolis: University of Minnesota Press, 1973), 83 according to Ibn Ǧubayr cited in Aḥmad

Ibn Ǧubayr includes the customary traditions[21] about Damascus in this section and continues:

> *In fact, wherever you look in all four directions, its bright, green foliage, laden with ripe fruit, holds your gaze. By Allah, they told the truth who said: 'If Paradise be on earth, Damascus must be it, if it is in heaven, Damascus can parallel and match it.*[22]

The beauty of Damascus also did not fail to win over European travelers. It is remarkable that its beauty is praised by them in a manner resembling

b. Muḥammad al-Maqqarī (at-Tilimsānī): *Nafḥ aṭ-ṭīb min ġuṣn al-Andalus ar-raṭīb wa-ḏikr waẓīrihā Lisān ad-Dīn Ibn al-Ḫaṭīb*, ed. Iḥsān ʿAbbās, 8 vols. (Bayrūt: Dār Ṣādir, 1968), 2: 386–387; see also Ibn Ǧubayr: *Riḥlat Ibn Ǧubayr*, ed. Ḥusayn Naṣṣār (al-Qāhira: Maktabat Miṣr, 1992), 386–387 and the translation of Ronald J. C. Broadhurst: *The Travels of Ibn Jubayr: being the chronicle of a Spanish moor concerning his journey to the Egypt of Saladin, the holy cities of Arabia, Baghdad the city of the Caliphs, the Latin kingdom of Jerusalem, and the Norman kingdom of Sicily* (London: Cape 1952), 271.

21 Ibn Ǧubayr transmits the tradition of al-Aṣmāʿī (d. 216/828), that there are three paradises on earth: 'The Damascus Ġūṭa, Balḫ River, and the Ubullah River'; further a tradition of al-Ḫwārizmī (d. ca. 232/850): *'The earthly paradises are four: The Ġūṭa of Damascus, the Vale of Suġd near Samarqand, the Vale of Bawwān and the Islet of Ubullah'*. Ibn Ǧubayr then refers to ancient records, that Damascus is revered as a birthplace of Abraham (on the mount al-Qāsiyūn), and as a refuge for Mary and her son (according to Q 25:52), and that Damascus was visited by Muhammad, where his eyes fell on the orchard-ringed multicolored city, compared with paradise' (see Hitti: *Capital Cities*, 82–84). Referring to Ibn Ǧubayr, the famous traveler Ibn Baṭṭūṭa (d. 770/1368 or 779/1377) enlarged the praise of Damascus, see *Riḥlat Ibn Baṭṭūṭa*, ed. Darwīš al-Ǧuwaydī (Bayrūt: al-Maktaba al-ʿAṣriyya, 2004), 1: 78–100 and 2: 298–300 (poetry about Damascus).

22 Hitti: *Capital Cities*, 84.

that of Arab scholars. Ludolph of Sudheim (1340),[23] for example, writes that

> *the city was noble and beautiful to an extent that it was difficult to find a city on earth that could surpass it. She is full of the delightfulness of earth, full of all commodities that human art can create, ... you can find a never-ending amount of golden jewelry, items made of silver, jewels, silk and all kinds of valuable textiles.*[24]

Common topoi of city panegyrics in poetry

City panegyrics adhere to the mode of classical Arabic love poetry and poetry of nature in *waṣf* (*ekphrasis*), *madḥ* (panegyric), and *hiǧā'/ḏamm* (dispraise, critique). Urban imagery, formerly foreign to the *qaṣīda*, found its way into poetry firstly in smaller parts of the *nasīb* and *raḥīl* sections, gradually ousting the old Arabic imagery of the desert-dwelling Bedouin and the virtues connected with it. However, the desert imagery did not entirely disappear, but the rise of Islam and processes of urbanization as well as changing actualities of life in large parts of the Islamic world caused a shift in classical motifs which were then expressed in the contrast

---

23 Ludolph of Sudheim visited Damascus between 1336 and 1341, during his pilgrimage to the Holy Land. The city was also praised in the same manner by Guillaume de Boldensele (i.e. Otto de Nyenhusen, d. 1339 in Cologne) and Jacques de Vérone (about 1335). For all these accounts, see Gérard Degeorge: *Damaskus*, [transl.] Jürgen Brankel (Wien: Verlag Turia + Kant, 2006), 1: 371; 2: 20 and Stefan Schröder: *Zwischen Christentum und Islam: Kulturelle Grenzen in den spätmittelalterlichen Pilgerberichten des Felix Fabri* (Berlin: Akademie Verlag, 2009), esp. 78–80.

24 Degeorge: *Damaskus*, 2: 20.

of nomadic and sedentary images or were used more figuratively (e.g., mystically) entering other sujets.[25] It was not before the expansion of the caliphate, that urban imagery formed an autonomous motif-ensemble within a *qaṣīda* eventually leading to separate city-poems.[26] This process is nearly the same as in antiquity, where the city-praise began with short epithets within rhetorical speech and progressed into the language of the arts (prose and poetry), with growing imagery as a subgenre.[27]

Although traditional Arabic literary criticism lacks a theory of city panegyrics, in practice it very much adheres to Menander's rules formulated in his treatises "Division of Epideictic Styles" (commonly *Diairesis*) and "On Epideictic Speeches" (commonly *Peri Epideiktikon*).[28] Even if we never find an application of the complete catalogue of the genos *laus urbis*, it was exercised extensively and applied modularly. In addition to topographical characteristics (habitat, climate, geography, etc.) puns on the names

---

25 For poetic examples of the nomadic-sedentary (Arabic: *al-bādī/al-ḥaḍar*) dichotomy in ʿAbbasid times, see Bayyud: *Die Stadt in der arabischen Poesie*, 191–205. See also Grunebaum: "Aspects of Arabic urban literature, mostly in the ninth and tenth centuries", 281–282.

26 Bayyud: *Die Stadt in der arabischen Poesie*, 5–15 lists some old Arabic and early Islamic verses with urban imagery. The first autonomous city-poem is according to Bayyud composed by ʿĀʾiša al-ʿUṯmāniyya in the period of the second Umayyad caliph al-Yazīd I (647–683), see *ibid.*, 15.

27 For parallels in the Arabic literary tradition, taking al-Ḥarīrī's *Maqāmāt* as an example, see von Grunebaum: "Observations on City Panegyrics", esp. 63–65. For the classics, see Weißhaar-Kiem: *Lobschriften und Beschreibungen ehemaliger Reichs- und Residenzstädte in Bayern bis 1800*, 13–23.

28 For his catalogue of city panegyrics, see *Menander Rhetor*, ed. with translation and commentary by Donald A. Russel and Nigel G. Wilson (Oxford: Clarendon Press, 1981). See also Weißhaar-Kiem: *Lobschriften und Beschreibungen ehemaliger Reichs- und Residenzstädte in Bayern bis 1800*, 14–17 and Laurent Pernot: *Epideictic Rhetoric: Questioning the Stakes of Ancient Praise* (Texas: University of Texas Press, 2015), esp. 11–12.

of cities and its derivatives were very common: e.g., *Šām* – *ša'm/šūm/ šā'ma* (bad omen), *šāma* (beauty spot), *šā'ma* (left side); Buḫāra – *ḫarā* (excrement), Balḫ – *baḫīl* (avarice), Istanbul – Islāmbūl/ol (where Islam is to be found / where Islam is plenty). The urban motif-inventory for Damascus is impressively large as there is almost nothing which did not receive poetic praise.

The following enumeration of urban topics varies considerably in the texts, depending on historical context, direction of praise or criticism and motivation of the writer, but among the most frequent topics for Damascus and most of the city panegyrics are:

a) *for the natural habitat*: landscape, soil, public gardens, recreational places, hills and valleys, mountains, plants, flowers, animals (especially doves), fruits (especially apples and grapes), ~fragrances, rivers

b) *for the climate*: seasons, fresh and healthy air, clouds, rain, snow, heat

c) *for the built urban environment*: protective walls, irrigation system quarters, markets, mosques, bazars, houses, palaces, *ḫāns*, miles, gates, endowment-buildings, schools, hospitals, tombs, infrequently: roads, streets

d) *cultural/social topics*: famous individuals, scholarship, mentalities of inhabitants (hostilities and hospitality, good or bad character), structure and mentality of urban quarters, religious coexistence, young men, old men, slaves, beauty of the people (body, hair, eyes, clothing) women, families, behavior of groups, guilds, festivities, taverns

e) *material culture*: handcraft markets, manufactured products (clothes (silk and brocade), swords and glass), guilds, fragrances, birds, food and cooking, wine

f) *administration topics* (domination, safety and protection): ruler, governor, castle, towers, military and security forces, parades

g) *religious topics*: scholarship, mosques, tombs, learning institutions, venerated persons and places, ascetics, judges and posts

h) *historical and intertextual topics*: *ḥadīṯs* concerning the city, quotations from the Qurʾān, conquest narratives, grounding narratives (esp. for Baghdad and Cairo), famous companions, merits of caliphs and sultans, dynasties (Umayyads), mystics, ar-Rūm, Franks, sayings, poems, disputes

i) *position of the city*: geographical specifics within a city-ensemble, within the kingdom, religious position (ranking).

Damascus toponyms

Almost every corner and every title of Damascus was object of a panegyric. The most common toponyms for Damascus are: *aš-Šaqrāʾ*; *al-Ġūṭā*; *an-Nayrab/ayn*; *ar-Rabwa*; *aš-Šaraf*; *al-Ǧabha*; *al-Mizza*; *Ǧillaq/Ǧilliq*; *al-Ḫaḍrāʾ*; *aṣ-Ṣāliḥiyya*; *al-Liwān*; *al-Maydān*. All of these distinctive places are also used as metonyms for Damascus/Šām in poetry.[29] In a few verses al-Maqqarī (992/1584 - 1041/1631) alludes to some of the chosen places and titles of Damascus, while asserting the reality of conventionalized comparisons: (meter: *kamil*; toponyms and epithets underlined)

أما دمشقُ لخضرةٌ   لعبتْ بألبابِ الخلائقْ

هِيَ بَهْجَتُ الدُّنيا التي   مِنْها بديعُ الحسْنِ رائِقْ

---

29 For these poems, see Muḥammad Ibn ar-Rāʿī (Ibn Ḫudāwirdī): *Al-Barq al-mutʾalliq fī maḥāsin Ǧilliq*, ed. Muḥammad Adīb al-Ǧādir (Dimašq: Maṭbūʿāt Maǧmaʿ al-Luġa al-ʿArabiyya bi-Dimašq 1429/2008) and Muḥammad al-Miṣrī: *ad-Dīwān ad-Dimašqī: šiʿr nuẓima fī Dimašq qadīman wa-ḥadīṯan* (Bayrūt: Dār al-Fikr al-Muʿāṣira, 1413/1991).

لله مِنْها الصالحيـ يةُ فاخرتْ بِذَوي الحَقائِقْ
والغُوطةُ الغناءُ حيَّـ يثٌ بالورودِ وبالشقائِقْ

Damascus is a verdant spot / that plays with all creatures' hearts.

She is the joy of the world and her amazing beauty is delightful.

(It is due to God that) aṣ-Ṣāliḥiyya is / proud of the bearers of the truths.[30]

The splendid Ġūṭa is equipped with roses and anemones.[31]

Aṣ-Ṣāliḥiyya is known for the many *salaf aṣ-ṣāliḥ* buried there. Together with *Ǧabal al-Qāsiyūn*, where the tombs of several thousand martyrs and prophets are believed to be, Arab encyclopedists like al-Yāqūt (574– 626/ 1179–1229) describe it as one of the most venerated places.[32] The toponyms appear mainly in the first hemistich, while in the second the poet enumerates their (positive) effects. Although the poet employs very dynamic phrases, the poem evokes the impression of a peaceful and calm beauty to emphasize Damascus' grace.

---

30 *Ḏawū l-ḥaqā'iq* refer to the tombs of the *as-salaf aṣ-ṣāliḥ* in general and the tomb of Ibn ʿArabī in particular.

31 Verses 1–4 of 9 of Aḥmad b. Muḥammad al-Maqqarī (at-Tilimsānī) in his *Nafḥ aṭ-ṭīb,* 1: 59–60; see also Muḥammad al-Miṣrī: *ad-Dīwān ad-Dimašqī*, 258. – Another poem of al-Maqqarī (*Nafḥ aṭ-ṭīb*, 1: 61) states about Damascus: *If you want to describe the beauties of the world, do not start with any city other than Damascus* (وإذا وصفتَ محاسنَ الدنيا فلا تبدأ بغير دمشق فيها أوّلا). Al-Maqqarī's poem is one of several poetic responses to the question of how to describe the city adequately. For the many other Damascus-related poems, divided into a praise and blame section, see volumes 1 and 2 in the same work (1: 58–69 and 2: 381–494).

32 See Nikita Elisséeff: "Ḳāsiyūn", in: *Encyclopaedia of Islam*, 2nd ed., 4: 724.

Damascus is sexy

Two particularly playful variations of the body imagery of Damascus divide the city's quarters erotically, the first in describing a masculine and the second, a feminine beauty. Ibn Nubāta's (686–768/1287–1366) impression of a day in Damascus is expressed in the following way: (meter: *rağaz*; toponyms underlined)

يَا حَبَّذا يَوِمي بِوادِي جِلَّقٍ   وفُرْجَتِي مَعَ الْغَزَالِ الحَالِي

مِنْ أَوَّلِ الجَبْهَةِ قد قَبَّلْتُهُ   مُرْتَشِفاً لِآخِرِ الخلخَالِ

> *What a day I had in the valley of Ğilliq, and what a joy (pleasant spectacle) with that ornamented gazelle!*
>
> *From the top of his forehead (toponym) I kissed him, with sipping sounds, until the bottom of his ankle rings (toponym).*[33]

The next *mawāliyā*-poem – ascribed to Ibrāhīm al-Miʿmār (d. 749/1348) – is introduced with the phrase 'may God pardon him!' by the historian Ibn

---

[33] *Dīwān Ibn Nubāta* in: Ms Nuruosmaniye 3802 fol. 221b, see also *Dīwān Ibn Nubāta*, ed. al-Qalqīlī, 419. The poem is cited in a slightly variant reading in Ibn Ṣaṣrā: *A Chronicle of Damascus (1389–1397)*, translated, edited and annotated by William M. Brinner (Berkeley: University of California Press, 1963), 209 [ar.158 b]. For details on Ibn Nubāta's work and life, see Thomas Bauer: "Dignity at Stake: Mujūn epigrams by Ibn Nubāta (686–768/1287–1366) and his contemporaries", in: *The Rude, the Bad and the Bawdy. Essays in honour of Professor Geert Jan van Gelder,* ed. Adam Talib, Marlé Hammond, Arie Schippers (Cambridge: Gibb Memorial Trust, 2014) 160–185; idem: "Ibn Nubātah al-Miṣrī (686–768/1287–1366): Life and Works. Part I: The Life of Ibn Nubātah", in: *Mamlūk Studies Review* 12 (2008), 1–35. – "Part II: The Dīwān of Ibn Nubātah", in: *Mamlūk Studies Review* (2008), 25–69.

Ṣaṣrā.[34] The poet arranges the quarters and suburbs of Damascus by using its toponyms in different figures of speech, which allude to the body of a well-shaped woman (line 4): (toponyms underlined)

لك يا دمشق شرف عالي و شهر الصوم

ونيربين وربوه عاليه في السوم[35]

وحسن جبهه ولك خلخال يسبي دَوْم

وتحت قلعه وجامع كم جمع من قوم

Thou hast, O Damascus (toponym), high dignity (epithet, toponym and tawriya), and (but) it is the month of fasting,

(thou hast) an-Nayrabayn (toponym; here also metaphorical for 'breasts') and a 'hill' (toponym, alluding to 'behind') of high value.

And a beautiful al-ǧabha (toponym of the quarter and tawriya for 'forehead'), and al-ḫalḫāl (toponym of the quarter and tawriya for 'ankles'), which forever captivate,

34 The poem, as it is cited in Ibn Ṣaṣrā: *A Chronicle of Damascus (1389–1397)*, 209 [ar.158 b] does not scan properly as a *mawāliyā*. For this reason, I have omitted the vocalisation provided in the edition. Ibn Ṣaṣrā probably erred in attributing the poem to Ibn al-Miʿmār, since it does not occur in the edited *Dīwān*. See *Der Dīwān des Ibrāhīm al-Miʿmār (gest. 749/1348-49). Edition und Kommentar*, ed. by Thomas Bauer et al. (Baden-Baden, Ergon: 2019).

35 An-Nayrabayn was divided into *an-Nayrab al-aʿlā*, situated between Yazīd and Ṯawrā rivers, and *an-Nayrab al-adnā*, located between Ṯawrā and Baradā rivers. See Taqī ad-Dīn al-Badrī: *Nuzhat al-anām fī maḥāsin aš-Šām,* ed. Ibrāhīm Ṣāliḥ (Damascus: Dār al-Bašāʾir, 2006), 82–83.

and "below the citadel" (toponym and a tawriya for 'nether region'), and a mosque which assemble how many people!

On its north side, the quarter *taḥt al-qal'a* (Under the Citadel) is – at least in Mamluk times – a nightly fairground for clowns, jugglers, conjurers and story tellers.[36] A comparable quarter to Cairo's Bāb al-Lūq, where Ibrāhīm al-Mi'mār lived and died. However, is not known if al-Mi'mār ever visited Damascus, in which case this may be praise given of a city only known through literary tradition and literary discourse via Ibn Nubāta.

Damascus as a paradise

Equating Damascus with paradise and eternity is one of the most frequently employed comparisons, which has prevailed up to our times. To give a negative example, when Damascus' rank is denied, this, however, affirms that there was already a discourse likening it to paradise:

دمشقُ كما كنتَ تَسمعُ جنّةٌ　　　أَلمْ تَرَها محفوفةً بالمكارهِ

Damascus, often you have heard that she is a paradise, don't you see that she is full of (lit.: surrounded by) detestable things?[37]

36 See Ross Burns: *Damascus. A History* (London: Routledge, 2007), 205.

37 This verse is attributed to Ibn al-Wardī (691/1291-749 /1348): *Dīwān Ibn al-Wardī*, ed. Aḥmad Fawzī al-Hayb (Kuwayt: Dār al-Qalam, 1407/1986), 123. However, the phrase *maḥfūfatun bi-l-makārihī* is known in *ḥadīṯ* literature (e.g., *ḥuffat al-ğanna bi-l-makārihi wa-ḥuffat an-nār bi-š-šahawāt.* "The Paradise is surrounded by hardships and the Hell-Fire is surrounded by temptations"), as al-Ğāhiẓ points to it: *a-wa-laysati l-nāru maḥfūfatan bi-š-šahawāt, a-wa-laysati l-ğannatu maḥfūfatan bi-l-makārih?* (in: al-Ğāhiẓ, *Rasā'il*, ed. Muḥammad Hārūn (al-Qāhira: Maktabat al-Ḫānğī, 1964), I: 287 (in: *Risāla fī nafy at-tašbīh*) and also the poet and chief qāḍī of Baghdad Ṣāliḥ b. 'Abd al-Quddūs (in: Ibn 'Abd Rabbih: *al-'Iqd al-farīd*, ed. Mufīd Muḥammad Qumayḥa

'Of not being paradise' does not mean the linear opposite (a contrary opposition), like being 'hell', but is instead a semantic specification of what belongs to paradise and what does not. A city of paradise promotes moral and pious manners, where what generates discord has no place. Therefore, a city's attitude towards foreigners is also a topic that can be used to heap blame on a city and question its paradisiacal rank. This is the case in the following poem, which uses a subtle irony, first to confirm the rank and then undermine it using the rhetorical figure of false praise (*ta'kīd aḏ-ḏamm bi-mā yušbih al-madḥ*):

دمشق جنّة الدنيا حقيقاً ولكن ليس تصلح للغريب

بها قومٌ لهم عددٌ ومجدٌ وصحبتهم تؤول إلى حروب

Damascus is really paradise on earth, / but she is not good for the stranger (here, the Andalusian poet from the West).

There are people, glorious and plenty in number, / and (but) their friendship leads to wars.[38]

Since the Ottoman conquest, Istanbul/Constantinople had also belonged to the group of cities competing for the rank of paradise. Because of the scriptural tradition, poetry and particularly the general pervasiveness of poetic imagery, Damascus' literary rank was already canonized. Even if

(Bayrūt: Dār al-Kutub al-ʿIlmiyya, 1404/1983), 2: 186 (v. 3 of 3): *wa-li-llāhi fī ʿarḍi s-samāwāti ǧannatun / wa-lākinna maḥfūfatun bi-l-makārihī*. For a positive attribution of Damascus to paradise, see Ibn Ǧubayr (quoted above). It was quite common to write praise and dispraise for the same subject, as a consequence of this, there are poems in which Damascus' rank is denied. For these, see al-Maqqarī: *Nafḥ aṭ-ṭīb,* 2: 381–494 and Bayyud: *Die Stadt in der arabischen Poesie*, 160–191 (174–175 for Damascus).

38 Verses 1–2 of 3 of al-Kātib Abū Bakr Muḥammad Ibn Qāsim, an Andalusian poet, cited in al-Maqqarī: *Nafḥ aṭ-ṭīb*, 2: 406.

an author denies a city a certain attribute, the very fact of denying it is thus already an admission that others consider this attribute to be applicable. Poets faced a challenge if they wanted to change the rank of priority, as in the case of Istanbul as the new imperial center. The Ottoman poet Nedīm (1681–1730) copes with this challenge, setting his city against prefigured imagery by almost crossing the boundaries of the religiously appropriate.

> *Holy Paradise! Is it under or above the city of Istanbul?*
>
> *My Lord, how nice is its atmosphere, its water and weather!*
>
> *Each of its gardens is a pleasing meadow,*
>
> *Each corner is fertile, a blossoming assembly of joy.*
>
> *It is not proper to exchange the city for the whole world.*
>
> *Or to compare its rose gardens to paradise!*[39]

---

[39] [Emphasis mine] Poem cited in Deniz Çalış-Kural: *Şehrengiz, Urban Rituals and Deviant Sufi Mysticism in Ottoman Istanbul* (London: Ashgate, 2014), 203. The *şehrengiz* (lit.: a city thriller) is a mostly Persian and Turkish poetic genre that emerged from Timurid times and initially about the beauties (young craftsmen) of a city and is not known in Arabic. However, the genre underwent many topical and formal transformations up to hymnodies for cities. Nearly every important Ottoman city in the Rumelia is the object of a *şehrengiz*. By now, we know about only one *şehrengiz* for an Arab city in the Ottoman language. It was composed for Aleppo in the16th century (see Yunus Kaplan: "Seyrī ve Halep Şehrengizi", in: *Divan Edebiyatı Araştırmalari Dergisi* 14 (2015), 67–92. The most widely used poetic form used in the *şehrengîz* genre was the *maṯnawī* (poem of rhymed couplets), however, the *qaṣīda* (ode), *rubāʿī* (quatrain, Arabic: *ḏūbayt*) and the *terci-i bent* or *terkib-i bent* forms (stanzaic long poem following the *ġazal* form, where each stanza is linked by a recurring *bayt* (*wāsiṭa/band*) with the same or a differing rhyme) were also used. For the tradition of this genre in general, see Michele Bernardini: "The masnavi-shahrashubs as Town Panegyrics: An International Genre in Islamic Mashriq", in:

Verses 2–4 confirm positive qualities of Istanbul using classical topics of city praise in combination with predicates, stressing the effect on the human soul, like: the atmosphere, water and weather are nice, the meadow-like gardens are pleasing, and the whole city is fertile, blossoming, and joyful. However, they also affirm, how paradise is described, i.e., what belongs to paradise.

While verses 2–4 affirm the qualities of the city, the poet goes beyond the paradise comparison by locating Istanbul in a sublime sphere (verses 1, 5 and 6). The rhetorical question concerning the position of paradise in the first verse is based on a reverted simile (Arabic: *at-tašbīh al-maqlūb/ mušabbah maqlūb*)[40] that preceded the question. As the hidden layer under a metonymy (*kināya*) a common simile like 'a city is like paradise' has been reverted into 'paradise is like the city or inferior to it'. Particularly in the reverse simile (*mušabbah maqlūb*), the share of tertium comparationis – usually borrowed from the qualities of the secundum comparationis – appears higher in the primum comparationis: Moreover, it is especially in the reverse simile that the rate of *tertium comparationis* – usually borrowed from the qualities of the *secundum comparationis* – becomes higher in the *primum comparationis*:

Erzählter Raum in Literaturen der islamischen Welt / Narrated Space in the Literature of the Islamic World, ed. Roxane Haag-Higuchi and Christian Szyska (Wiesbaden: Harrassowitz Verlag, 2001), 81–94; Peter de Bruijn (et al.): "Shahrangīz", in: *Encyclopaedia of Islam*, 2nd ed., 9: 212; Barış Karacasu: "Türk Edebiyatında Şehrengizler", in: *Türkiye Araştırmaları Literatür Dergisi* 5 (2007), 259–313; Bayram Ali Kaya: "Şehrengiz", in: *DİA*, 38: 461–462 (with further references) and Walter G. Andrews and Mehmet Kalpaklı: *The Age of Beloveds: Love and the Beloved in Early-Modern Ottoman and European Culture and Society* (Durham: Duke University Press, 2005), esp. 32–58.

40 For some further examples, see the section about the *mufāḫara*-part in this study.

In the reverted simile the rate of the tertium comparationis – usually borrowed from the *secundum comparationis* – is higher in the *primum comparationis*:

at-tašbīh al-mufaṣṣal (complete simile)

> Damascus (primum comparationis) is like a paradise (secundum comparationis) – regarding her beauty (tertium comparationis)

at-tašbīh al-maqlūb (reverted simile)

> Paradise has stolen her beauty from Damascus (former primum comparationis; the 'rate' of beauty is higher in Damascus).

It is evident, that a reverted simile is only possible when a simile has already been established. Furthermore, Nedīm's poem offers an intertextual adoption from a 45-line poem of ʿImād ad-Dīn al-Iṣfahānī (d. 597/1201) about the merits of Damascus,[41] himself following the example of aṭ-Ṭarābulusī (d. 545/1153).[42] Beside this intertextual linkage, it is very likely that the older Greek tradition of comparing Constantinople to paradise was known to Nedīm.[43] As in the Islamic tradition, Constantinople's rank is highly praised in Greek texts, bearing epithets like: *'the eye of the*

---

41 Verse 12 of 45: وإنَّ مَنْ باعَ كلَّ العُمرِ مُقْتَنعاً ... بساعةٍ في ذَراها غيرُ مَغْبونِ "If someone would sell his life, / to spend only one hour on her soil, he would not have been deceived (for goods received)", cited in Bayyud: *Die Stadt in der arabischen Poesie*, 125–126.

42 See Bayyud: *Die Stadt in der arabischen Poesie*, 125.

43 Michele Bernardini notes that the Turks adopted the Byzantine *Patria* material on a large scale (see "The masnavi-shahrashubs as Town Panegyrics", 83).

world', 'second or *new Rome'*, the *'second paradise'* (after Eden), *'Eden on earth'* and even a *'more beautiful paradise than the heavenly'*.[44]

The latter epithet also underlies the next poem, where the paradise trope is used to describe Constantinople.[45] Here, however, it is not an implicit comparison with Damascus but an explicit reference to Mecca that exalts the city.

If Adam had ever seen that bejeweled location

The heart would have forgotten the Paradise

Every one of its mosques is a divine reflection of Ka'be [...]

Being a divine reflection of the Kaʿba provides the poet with a justification for placing his own city superior to paradise. Obviously, it was easier for the Turkish poet to rank paradise lower than the sacred site of Islam. As it was written during the age of Sultan Süleyman or even before, these verses convey a highly political message about legitimizing Ottoman power.

'Good' and 'Bad City' contrast

Criticizing and contrasting one's own city with others clarifies which aspects are constituting factors of an ideal or good city in a poetic sphere. A poet may elevate a city by affirming the high rank of other cities and countries in order to reaffirm its own position or in order to enter the arena of competition: (meter: *basīṭ*)

44 Rhoby: "Stadtlob und Stadtkritik in der byzantinischen Literatur", 286–289.

45 Poem in an anonymous *şehrengiz* written before 1566 in Çalış-Kural: *Şehrengiz, Urban Rituals and Deviant Sufi Mysticism in Ottoman Istanbul*, 130–131.

دعْ عنكَ حضرة بغداد وبهجتها ولا تعظم بلاد الفرس والصين

فما على الأرضِ قطرٌمثل قرطبة وما مشى فوقها مثل ابن حمدين

Do not mention Baghdad with all its glittering magnificence;/

And do not magnify the lands of Persia and China.

Nowhere on earth [is there] a spot like Cordova. /

Nor in the world a man like Ibn Hamdun.[46] [read Ibn Ḥamdīn]

The poem informs us that these lands are already over-praised and although rejected by the poet, worthy of a simile, just to intensify the contrasting effect, in order to boost Cordova. There is also an important second feature: For China, there is no established poetic imagery, besides the motif of a prosperous civilization, and that of being far away in the East. It marks the utmost end of the world in poetic reality.[47] When we reverse the enumeration towards Cordova, we see that China, Persia and Baghdad refer to the direction: East towards West, i.e. to Cordova, and from the abstract blurry beauty of China towards the more concrete, i.e. Cordova again.

46 Distich of an anonymous poet, cited in al-Maqqarī (at-Tilimsānī), Aḥmad b. Muḥammad: *Nafḥ aṭ-ṭīb*, 1: 459. The translation is given according to Pascual de Gayangos: *The history of the Mohammedan dynasties in Spain* (London: Oriental Translation Fund, 1840), 1: 202 and 483. De Gayangos reads *banī Ḥamdīn*, but this would be unmetrical and ungrammatical (*banī Ḥamdīn* would have required *amṯālu*).

47 Another poetic reference for China is given in al-Iṣfahānī's cited poem in verse 10: "*From Egypt to the end of China, there is no city (lit. I do not see any) that resembles her, regarding the beauty.*" (See Bayyud: *Die Stadt in der arabischen Poesie*, 125).

Another simpler contrast, which states Baghdad's merits as superior to those of Damascus, is given in ʿUmāra Ibn ʿAqīl's (d. 239/853) poem: (verses 1–4 of 7)

> *Have you ever seen in any corner of the world / a tranquil abode like Baghdad?*
>
> *Here, life is pure, green, and fresh; / in other places life is neither gentle nor cool.*
>
> *Life here is longer, the food is wholesome; / indeed, parts of the earth are better than others.*
>
> *God commanded that no Caliph will pass away / there; He decrees whatever He desires. A stranger can sleep here; unlike Damascus / where a stranger cannot close his eyes.*[48]

The poet an-Nawāǧī (d. 849/1455) boasts of his city (Cairo) by belittling Damascus and giving it a voice of its own. The reader, however, must consider that the rival has to be at least of the same rank as Cairo. The contrast of the bow (i.e. the power of Cairo) and the arrow (i.e. the arrow

48 [Emphasis mine; for the rhetoric figure of litotes see ch. "Inverting rhetorical devices"] The poem is translated by Reuven Snir: *Baghdad. The City in Verse* (Cambridge, MA: Harvard University Press, 2013), 93; see also Yāqūt: *Buldān* (ed. Bayrūt: Dār Ṣādir, 1397/1977), 1: 460–461 and the introductory chapter of al-Ḫaṭīb al-Baġdādī: *Tārīḫ Baġdād*, ed. Baššār ʿAwwād Maʿrūf (Bayrūt: Dār al-Ġarb al-Islāmī 1422/2001), 1: 355 and 1: 377 (meter: *ṭawīl*). In the oldest source *Aḫbār al-quḍāh* by Ibn Ḥayyān Wakīʿ (repr. Beirut: ʿĀlam al-Kutub, n. d.), 3: 299–300, with only four verses, the poem is attributed to the chief *qāḍī* of Baghdad Aḥmad Ibn Abī Dawūd b. Ǧarīr al-Iyādī (entry on him *idem*, 294–300). – Unlike Ibn ʿAqīl's critique, al-Qāḍī al-Fāḍil (529–596/1135–1200), the head of Ṣalāḥ ad-Dīn's chancery, states in favor of the Damascene hospitality (verse 1 of 8): "*Damascus is a paradise, where the stranger forgets about his homeland*", cited in al-Miṣrī: *ad-Dīwān ad-Dimašqī*, 22.

for the fleeing Damascus) illustrates a nice pun using the toponyms *as-sahm* and *qaws ar-rawḍa*, which are both recreational places: (meter: *mağzū' al-ḫafīf*)

مصرُ قالتْ دمشقُ لا   تفتخرْ قطّ بِاسْمِها

لو رأتْ قوسَ روضتي   منه راحتْ بِسَهمِها

Egypt (Cairo) said: 'Damascus / just takes pride in her name.

If she saw the bow of my garden (toponym of the Rawḍa-island), / she would go away with her arrow' (sahm: toponym in Damascus).[49]

The rivalry of cities is itself a topic in poetry. Apparently, the next poet delivers a religiously appropriate solution to the long-lasting competition between cities. He refers to a *ḥadīṯ* (rhetoric figure of *taḍmīn:* using a scriptural reference, cento),[50] commanding the balance be held (وَخَيرُ الأُمورِ

[49] Poem cited in Ibn Iyās: *Die Chronik des Ibn Ijās*, ed. Mohamed Mostafa (Stuttgart: Steiner, 1975), I,1: 272; idem: *Nuzhat al-umam fī 'ağā'ib wa-l-ḥikam*, ed. Muḥammad 'Izb (Cairo: Madbūlī, 1995), 38 and al-Maqqarī: *Nafḥ aṭ-ṭīb*, 2: 404 [old ed. 1: 739].

[50] The *ḥadīṯ*-text is varied, in this case an-Nābulusī designates the figure *talwīḥ* (intimation, hinting), see *The Arch Rhetorician or the Schemer's Skimmer. A Handbook of Late Arabic badī' drawn from 'Abd al-Ghanī an-Nābulsī's Nafaḥāt al-Azhār 'alā Nasamāt al-Asḥār*, summarized and systematized by Pierre Cachia (Wiesbaden: Harrassowitz, 1998), no: 169 and 171, where Cachia translates the term as "dispersal".

أَوْسَاطُهَا – following the middle way is a virtue), which is also a common saying ascribed to Socrates and Aristotle: (meter: *rağaz*)

في حلَبٍ وشامِنا ومصرَ طالَ اللَّغَطْ

فقلتُ قولَ مُنْصِفٍ خيرُ الأمورِ الوسَطْ

A lot of noise (idle prattle) has been produced about Aleppo, our Damascus, and Cairo.

I said, as someone who speaks fairly: 'Take the middle!'[51]

Behind these lines the poet conceals but nevertheless states his preference for Damascus by using a possessive pronoun (our Šām) and by ordering the cities in the north-south axis, where Damascus is automatically the (geographical) golden mean.

The Iraqi poet Muwaffaq ad-Dīn Ibn Abī l-Ḥadīd (born 590/1194; died 656/1258 shortly after the siege of Baghdad by the Mongols) offers a more moderate solution for the Syrian cities, probably because he was worried about the same fate that overtook Baghdad: (meter: *basīṭ*)

تقاسمت بي أقطار البلاد فقد أصبحتُ مجتمعاً في زي منشعب

في القدس عزمي وجسمي في دمشق بلا قلب وقلبي مع الأحباب في حلب

The cities (lit. regions) have divided my body amongst themselves / thus I found myself (my parts) pieced together in a ragged cloth.

---

51 Anonymous poem cited in al-Maqqarī: *Nafḥ aṭ-ṭīb*, 2: 405 and in Hasan Kujjah & Mohammad Kujjah: *Ḥalab aš-Šahbāʾ fī ʿuyūn aš-šuʿarāʾ* (Leiden: Brill, 2022), vol. 1: *Ḥalab fī š-šiʿr al-qadīm: bayna l-qarn as-sābiʿ li-l-milād wa-maṭlaʿ al-qarn al-ʿišrīn*, 395.

> *In al-Quds there is my vigor (will), whereas my body is in Damascus without / the heart, and my heart is with my friends in Aleppo.*[52]

The metaphor of the divided body, though centered again in Damascus, expresses the poet's concern with the whole of Syria as an entity, where neither of the cities is complete without the others. However, the partitioning of the human body is trisected along the south-north-axis (in this case al-Quds, Damascus, and Aleppo). The parts of the body attributed to each of these cities correspond to will (*ʿazm*), body (*ğism*) and emotion (*qalb*). To emphasize the inner struggle, how the poet feels torn between his desires and needs he uses the digressive technique of *al-ğamʿ maʿa t-taqsīm wa-t-tafrīq* (*connection-cum-division* and *separation*), which is also indicated lexically in the first verse with the words *taqāsamat, muğtamiʿan* and *ziyy munšaʿab*.

52 Quṭb ad-Dīn al-Yunīnī: *Ḏayl Mirʾāt az-zamān* (Hyderabad: Osmania Oriental Publications Bureau, 1954), 1: 104–108 for the author and the year 656/1258, for the poem, see 108.

Modes of panegyric

Praise and its inversion – critique and its inversion

If we explore the aforementioned examples further, we can see that praise can be achieved by:

- counting positive attributes either seen independently or in relation to other cities,
- humiliating/lowering the object of comparison (in our case the other city),
- enumerating the negative attributes that are missing from the city (e.g. in the form of a *litotes*),
- by rhetorical figures, which produce irony and satire: the device of *ta'kīd al-madḥ bi-mā yušbih aḏ-ḏamm* (false blame).

All of this holds true for critique (*ḏamm*) if it is inverted:

- counting negative attributes either seen independently or in relation to other cities,
- enlarging (the faults) of the object of comparison (in our case the other city),
- enumerating the positive attributes that are missing from the city (by negation),
- using the rhetorical device of *ta'kīd aḏ-ḏamm bi-mā yušbih al-madḥ* (false praise).

Motivations of the poet

When looking for the reasons for poets to praise or lament a city, we can observe different motivations for praise, blame and description:

(a) Urban life provides ample opportunities for a poet to expand motifs with comparisons and metaphors e.g., for love poetry. Subsequently the personified city as a new object joins the group of the adored, i.e.

man, woman, youngling and slave. Or, the poet participates in a specific discourse about a contested precedent (e.g. poem: *Do not mention Baghdad, ...*).

(b) The poet needs to express his personal impression either by enumerating several characteristics or highlighting just a single one. In praising a scholar of the city, the famous Syrian poet Manǧak Pasha (d. 1080/1669) writes: (verse 2 of 2)

وَلَولا أَن دارَك في دمشق　　　لَمَا افتَخَرَت دمشق على البِلاد

If your house were not in Damascus, / Damascus could not boast herself in front of other cities.[53]

(c) The poet considers himself to be the voice of society, as was the case at the judicial court in Damascus: There were four chief judges appointed as representatives of the four schools of law (*maḏhab*) at the same time. This was a novelty in Damascus, but when they started to compete with each other they caused an atmosphere of resentment among the population. Coincidentally these judges all had the name Šams ad-Dīn. The poets jumped at this opportunity. The following poem uses a nice pun with the figures *ṭibāq* (here *ẓalām* 'darkness' / *šams* 'bright') and *tawriya* (double entendre with the words *šams* for the names and the sun):[54] (meter: *~muǧtaṯṯ*)

---

53 Manǧak Bāšā: *Dīwān*, ed. Muḥammad Bāsil ʿUyūn as-Sūd (Dimašq: Manšūrāt al-Hayʾa al-ʿĀmma as-Sūriyya li-l-Kitāb, 2009), no: 101 (206).

54 Poem cited in Šihāb ad-Dīn Abū Šāma: *ar-Rawḍatayn fī aḫbār ad-dawlatayn an-nūriyya wa-ṣ-ṣalāḥiyya wa-yalīhi aḏ-ḏayl ʿalā tarāǧim riǧāl al-qarnayn as-sādis wa-s-sābiʿ* (Bayrūt: Dār al-Kutub al-ʿIlmiyya, 1422/2002), 5: 357 with other poems on the same topic like the following *mufrad* verse: "Our judges, all of them are 'suns', but we live in 'the deepest darkness'" (قضاتنا كلهم شموس ... ونحن في أكثف الظلام).

أهلُ دمشقَ استرابوا   من كثرةِ الحكامِ

إذ همْ جميعاً شموسٌ   وحالهم في ظلامِ

The Damascenes are confused by the number of their judges.

All of them are suns. But they (the Damascenes) are in the dark.

(d) In the case of praising or rebuking a ruler, as well as to critique domination, the city may serve as a welcome proxy. A particularly telling example of the discourse about a ruler and the ethics of power can be found in al-Maqrīzī's account of the year 762/1361 in Cairo: After the collapse of a minaret on a *maktab as-sabīl*, and the loss of 300 lives, most of them orphans who were reciting the Qur'ān, the public started to accuse the sultan (Ḥasan) and saw this incident as a warning about the impending downfall of the state. The people must have been upset to such an extent that the poet catches the sentiments and tries to offer an explanation, while putting some energy in the rhetorical figure of *ḥusn at-ta'līl* (using a fanciful cause) apparently to shield the sultan from blame: The minaret has fallen, not because it was the fault of the builder, but because she (*manāra*) was emotionally affected by listening to the Qur'ān recitation at her feet and so plummeted to the ground. Then the poet gives another reason, while moving to the praise-section of the poem: she tumbled to earth because the sultan, her beloved, was absent, and she became despondent and threw herself out of passion. The last section tries to combine the two unrelated motivations in presenting the good deeds of the sultan ironically.

(8) لاَ يَعْتَرِي البُؤسُ بَعْدَ اليومِ مَدْرَسَةً   شُيِّدَتْ بِنْيَانُهَا بِالعِلْمِ وَالعَمَل

(9) وَدُمْتَ حَتَّى تَرَى الدُّنْيَا بِهَا امْتَلأَتْ   عِلْمًا فَلَيْسَ بِمِصْرَ غيرُ مُشْتَغِلِ

From today, harm will strike no madrasa that is built with knowledge and practical skill.

May you live long enough, that you may see the world filled with knowledge, / – for no one in Egypt is not busy with it (in seeking knowledge or busy with talking about the event).[55]

When we invert the last verses, we read a piece of advice for the normative, righteous and correct deeds of a ruler, and get an idea of approved modes of public demands on his office (as a ruler), and therefore what the rituals of give and take were between ruler and public. Together with Martyn Smith's analysis of this poem,[56] we can assume that poetry reflects, within its codified language and devices, the discourse of power, state and social practice. It is perhaps the most important medium of political discourse and social memory.

55 The meter is *basīṭ*. For the Arabic text, see the appendix of this study.

56 A full translation is given in Martyn Smith: "Finding Meaning in the City. al-Maqrīzī's Use of Poetry in the Khiṭaṭ", in: *Mamluk Studies Review* 16 (2012), 154. However, I had to make some minor emendations in verse 8 and 9.

Label ranking

Ranking in the Qurʾān and other textual sources

Expansions of the body metaphor, which signify the city as a product, a brand and a stage of performance are somewhat more recent. The city has to compete with others in order to gain a place in the order of things. This city branding provides opportunities for a huge sector in the modern marketing industry. The sector is quite new but the approach had already become familiar in Arab Islamic culture. Cities often received markers (today we would call them labels) because of literary 'ascriptions'. If these markers were successful, they prevailed and stuck to the city like the material from which the city was built. Sometimes they even endured longer than the city they were applied to, as in the case of Baghdad. Hardly anything more than a 'stone' of remembrance survived from the round city of Baghdad (*al-madīna al-mudawwara*). Even the frequently used epithet *madīnat as-salām* (The City of Peace) has become highly anachronistic from the time of its foundation up to our own. The title 'City of peace' signifies a mode and an ideal of rule. The 'Round City' represents al-Manṣūr's claim to power. The entire world revolves around this city.

Not too much value should be placed on this ideological and religious concept, while it should also not be entirely ignored. From a religious perspective, Baghdad is not a holy city. Therefore, and because neither the Qurʾān nor tradition points in any way towards Baghdad, it cannot occupy a place in the *ḥadīṯ*-based religious ranking of cities. Receiving the name 'city of peace' or 'salvation' seems to be a strategy to compensate for 'having missed-out' on the religious ranking. Besides religiously, this ranking is also based on the old Arab tradition of praise (*madḥ; faḫr*). In later periods religious and secular rankings were amalgamated.

The religiously based marking, differentiating, and ranking find their evidence in the term and derivatives of *f-ḍ-l* (*faḍala* ~ to be superior, *faḍḍala* ~

to show preference for, *faḍl* ~ surplus, grace, favor, merit).[57] According to the Qurʾān, God grants his favor and a livelihood as he wishes, but he elevates some before others. He gave some a higher rank than others: وَاللّٰهُ فَضَّلَ بَعْضَكُمْ عَلَىٰ بَعْضٍ فِي الرِّزْقِ – *And God has preferred some of you over others in provision* (Q 16:71). The verse shows that the secular order of things is not based on equality but on its opposite. An important consequence of this is that inequality has to be seen as a blessing by God, it is His grace, as stated in Q 49:13: يَا أَيُّهَا النَّاسُ إِنَّا خَلَقْنَاكُمْ مِنْ ذَكَرٍ وَأُنْثَىٰ وَجَعَلْنَاكُمْ شُعُوبًا وَقَبَائِلَ لِتَعَارَفُوا – *O mankind! We have created you male and female and have made you nations and tribes that ye may know one another.*[58]

Why is such a high value put on the *faḍīla*? These rankings obtained special significance immediately after the death of the Prophet and the conflicts that arose during his succession. The method of selecting the first rightful caliphs is done according to said principle. The legitimacy of their caliphate (at least in later writings) was supported by the argument that they were *afḍal* ("more excellent", "superior") than others.

The argument about rank – in order to elevate claims in this new religious order – permeates the entire history of early Islam and is not limited to persons or tribes but is also applied to regions and cities. In this way cities and provinces increase their relevance as bases of a new community, as cornerstones of political parties and military centers.[59] The collections of

57 For a detailed discussion of the term, see Meir Max Bravmann: *The Spiritual Background of Early Islam: Studies in Ancient Arab Concepts* (Leiden: Brill, 2009), e.g., 175–177, 237–239, 243–247 and Gruber: Verdienst und Rang, 9–21.

58 Further Qurʾānic references are Q 2:47 and 122; Q 7:140; Q 45:46 (Israelites); Q 4:34 (women) and different topics in Q 2:253; Q 6:83 and 165; Q 12:76 and Q 43:32.

59 Gruber: *Verdienst und Rang*, 49–51 and 60–61.

tradition usually contain voluminous *manāqib-faḍā'il* chapters, which influenced later poetry concerning cities and vice versa and emerged into several distinct *faḍā'il*-works about regions and cities. In her study of Ibn 'Asākir's (d. 571/1176) history of Damascus, Zayde Antrim concludes regarding the genre of *faḍā'il* works and the discourse of place:

> *Furthermore, as expressions of local pride, these dictionaries allowed Muslims to celebrate the contribution made in their town to the sustenance of the most authoritative body of knowledge, after the Qur'an, in Islam. [... W]hile Ibn 'Asākir's faḍā'il claimed both sacred and secular distinctions for Damascus. Thus, Damascus emerges from these pages as a living, breathing city that could boast a powerful political past, monumental architecture, holy sites, and a thriving economy.*[60]

The genre of the *faḍā'il* draws from religious writings and religious tradition and is generally of a pious nature. In return and thanks to its fertile and adaptable structure, however, it feeds other genres like historiography, biography, travelogue and in general the *adab* literature. To be in any way mentioned in the *ḥadīṯ* – if not in the Qur'ān – is a reason for pride and elevating status claim. It is not surprising that later, relatively weak traditions were utilized for such purposes. Mecca as the birthplace of the prophet, place of the first revelation, and central holy place has an undeniable *faḍīla*. The same is true for Medina – both places are men-

---

[60] Zayde Antrim: "Ibn 'Asākir's Representations of Syria and Damascus in the Introduction to the Ta'rīkh Madīnat Dimashq", in: *IJMES* 38 (2006), 109–129, citations from 109 and 117.

tioned in the Qurʾān.[61] However, Egypt also wants to keep up: al-Maqrīzī explains proudly that the fact that God mentions it twenty times in his precious book, be it directly or indirectly, was part of Egypt's numerous *faḍāʾil*.[62] Damascus cannot compete in the same regard to the Qurʾān, but the books of the *faḍāʾil* aš-Šām surpass all other areas with regard to number and genre. Ar-Rabaʿī (d. 444 /1052) highlights some common merits of aš-Šām such as the following:

- *The piety of the Syrians is shown by the fact that Syria has the most saints, ascetics, and mosques.*[63]
- *God divided the good into ten equal parts. He placed nine tenths in Syria and divided the remaining part among the other countries.* [the text continues with the 'evil' in the reverse order].[64]
- *If aš-Šām is ruined, there will be no good in my umma.*[65]

Corresponding to the ranks determined as part of creation, cities and regions not favored by the prophet's word (i.e. cities that are not distinguished by a religious *faḍīla*), seek to compensate for their peripheral rank either by over-expanding the interpretation of references by exploiting rather weak traditions, or proudly displaying their achievements and deeds in the name of religion and the community. This is true for Baghdad

61 Q 6:92; Q 48:24 and for Medina, see Q 9:101 and 120 and Q 33:13. For the long tradition of literary debates between Mecca and Medina, see fn. 76 in this study.

62 Gruber: *Verdienst und Rang*, 55.

63 Abū l-Ḥasan ʿAlī ar-Rabaʿī: *Faḍāʾil aš-Šām wa-Dimašq*, ed. Ṣalāḥ ad-Dīn al-Munaǧǧid (Damascus: Maṭbūʿāt al-Maǧmaʿ al-ʿIlmī al-ʿArabī bī-Dimašq, 1950), no: 76 and Gruber: *Verdienst und Rang*, 71.

64 Ar-Rabaʿī: *Faḍāʾil aš-Šām wa-Dimašq*, no: 6 and Gruber: *Verdienst und Rang*, 71.

65 Ar-Rabaʿī: *Faḍāʾil aš-Šām wa-Dimašq*, no: 15 and Gruber: *Verdienst und Rang*, 71.

and for Basra. The praise of Basra, as a newcomer among the cities, offers a particularly telling example of this, and of the awareness of one's region and belonging. The famous composer of the *Maqāmāt*, al-Harīrī (d. 516/1122) integrates a rather weak tradition of the prophet into this praise of Basra. His (anti-)hero Abū Zayd addresses the Basrians on the virtues of their city:

> *Your country (Baṣra) is the most eminent of countries in purity, the richest of them in natural gifts, the widest in expanse, and the most fertile in pasture grounds. She boasts over them the correctest qibla, the broadest stream, the greatest number of rivers and date-palms, the most exquisite beauty in detail and aggregate, being the gateway into the sacred land, fronting the gate (of the Ka'ba) and the station (of Abraham). [...] A city based on God-fearing that was never tainted by fire temples, no idol had ever been circled around and its inhabitants prostrated themselves before nobody but the Almighty on its soil!*[66]

Inverting rhetorical devices

In the praise of Basra presented above, the positive statements confirm religiously motivated urban ideals such as purity, God-fearing, being equipped with 'sacred/pious' places, treasures of wisdom, bearers of knowledge and the presence of many worshippers. But the negative statements, which are a part of the concealed mockery of Mecca, also represent positive ideals behind them: if we invert the negatives (*never tainted...; no idol had ever ...; prostrated... before nobody but...*), they indicate praise of Basra.

66 [Emphasis mine] Translated by Grunebaum "Observations on City Panegyrics in Arabic prose", 63–64.

A poem by Ibn Dahhān al-Mawṣilī (d. 581/1185) concerning Damascus offers a similar example. In addition to utilizing the paradise motif, the poet expresses praise by stressing the absence of negatives: (verse 25 of 39)

ونحن في جنَّةٍ لا ذاق ساكنُها   بأساً ولا عرفت بؤساً مغانيها

> *We are in a Paradise whose inhabitants / do not taste adversity nor do its dwellers know sorrow (lit.: do not taste misery and its dwellings no sorrow).*[67]

By negating the terms 'adversity' and 'sorrow' – and also through a reverse attribution of animate and inanimate nouns to indicate that both human beings and the built environment of the city are intended – the verse offers its positive statement, namely the poetic ideal of a good city whose inhabitants live happily and securely. Therefore, we receive the poetical message through what is expressed in affirmative speech (*The city is ... xyz* (e.g., *beautiful*)) or through its denial in the litotic form of *the city has no*(*t*) + *negative term* (e.g., *adversity/misery/sorrow*). The amount of meaning that is poetically not expressed or mentioned is huge, but comprehensible, if we consider the rules of poetic speech, especially in its classical usage, as well as the fact that a positive statement always has to precede its negation. Even a linear negation like '*Damascus is not like paradise*', is within the poetic discourse of paradise, a deceptive affirmation of the rank formerly and generally attributed to it. In philosophy and in speculative theology, this kind of speech is called *apophatic* (e.g.: knowing God, by what he is not) as a negative theology in contrast to *kataphatic* (positive theology).[68] Further, the negation might not be inherent to posi-

---

67 For the full poem, see al-Miṣrī: *ad-Dīwān ad-Dimašqī*, 441–443.

68 These terms correspond to the Arabic *īǧāb* and *salb* in theological and philosophical discourse. As a rhetorical device, these terms also occur within the classification of the *antithesis* e.g., *aṭ-ṭibāq al-īǧābī* and *aṭ-ṭibāq as-salbī*.

tive statements in the language of logic and is also not entirely unproblematic. This is, however, possible in poetic language because a comparison of city A with city B that stresses their common aspect(s) also marks their differences (A is in the end not B). In summary, a literary comparison can be converted to shed light on what is poetically not said, and the comparison (*tašbīh*) in the end marks the difference and inequality in the language of the arts, as such a comparison presents the aesthetics of difference.

City-slam

City-slam as a parody of the debate genre

In the poetic and historical discourse of urbanity the city served as a tool for gaining and granting honor and dignity.[69] In Islamic culture, as in antiquity, honor was a currency and was put onto the market to accumulate value. Hence it was never stable and ever open to be challenged in competition.[70] As the pre-Islamic poetic tradition testifies "*Arabs were fond of boasting of all that constituted their honour (ʿirḍ), i.e. of everything that contributed to their ʿizza (power).*"[71]

The preceding paragraphs contained a discussion of city panegyrics in which a city is praised and blamed for one and the same issue, and where cities are contrasted in poetry and prose, either to boast about their own city or to give her a rank or deny the other city any rank at all. It is a discourse of space, and its annexation is for special purposes. One of the most playful genres where this ranking is contested is within debate literature, the *mufāḫara* (also *munāẓara, muḥāwara*).

69 See, for example, the *ḥadīṯ* based *faḍāʾil*, promoting the good qualities of groups, regions, and cities as a means to carry claims. See Wagner: "Munāẓara", in: *Encyclopaedia of Islam*, 2nd ed., 7: 565–568.

70 For a substantial discussion of the currency of honor in the Greco-Roman tradition, which in many aspects is applicable to the Islamic world, see Lendon: *Empire of honour: The Art of Government in the Roman World*, esp. chapters 1 and 2.

71 Wagner: "Mufākhara, [1]", in: *Encyclopaedia of Islam*, 2nd ed., 7: 308–309.

Originally a more scholarly genre for disputing academic topics, the *munāẓara* found its way into *adab* literature quite early.[72] As a literary genre, where more secular topics were contrasted, the *munāẓara* is a struggle for precedence and glory. In several aspects the rhetorical devices and purposes are the same as in the *faḫr*-section (self-praise, praise of the possessions and the tribe) of a *qaṣīda*.[73] The *munāẓara* may be composed in prose or verse or in a combination of both. As Ewald Wagner explains:

> [...] *two or more living or inanimate beings appear talking and competing for honor. The result of the competition depends on the discretion of the poet: a participant may declare himself defeated of his own free will, or the rivals may reach an understanding and recognise each other's equivalence. They may, however, also call in an arbitrator, who then awards victory to one participant or declares that both, or eventually all, are of equal standing. Finally, there may also surprisingly appear in the end a new competitor who claims victory.*[74]

Some early examples can be found in al-Ǧāḥiẓ in the *Kitāb Mufāḫarat al-ǧawārī wa-l-ġilmān* or in his *Kitāb al-Ḥayawān* for contests between a rooster and a dove, and sheep and goats, where the subjects, which are not usually opponents, were represented by a third person (*ṣāḥib)*. The contest between spring and autumn in *Salwat al-ḫarīf bi-munāẓarat ar-rabīʿ*

---

72 In poetry, a disputation between inanimate beings is found for the first time with the ʿAbbāsid poet al-ʿAbbās b. al-Aḥnaf (d. after 193/808), who makes heart and eye blame one another for the poet's love.

73 See Bichr Farès: "Mufākhara, [2]", in: *Encyclopaedia of Islam*, 2nd ed., 7: 309–310.

74 See Wagner: "Munāẓara", in: *Encyclopaedia of Islam,* 2nd ed.

wa-l-ḫarīf – obviously incorrectly ascribed to al-Ǧāḥiẓ – presents a fully developed *munāzara*, where the subjects speak for themselves. In poetry the fully developed *munāẓara* has been shown to exist since the 4th/10th century.[75]

In the didactic disputes, it was not primarily a matter of finding the truth regarding the *questio* or controversy, but of convincing the opponent of the greatest possible probability which one believes to have found. The dialogic structure of this genre was variously used for different topics based on a contest between two (natural) opponents for precedence regarding their qualities. As a consequence of vaunting their qualities and exposing the rival's faults, the debates were charged emotionally. However, the conception of 'opponents' differed widely. There are sometimes more than two opponents and, besides natural opposites (like male/female; black/white; human/animal and body/soul), there is more often a debate between 'similars' like rose and narcissus. In the case of city debates, however, there are hardly natural opposites, as the cities' rivalry was either feigned or had emerged from literary and cultural discourse.[76]

---

75 References are provided by Wagner: "Munāẓara"; see also Gelder: "The Conceit of Pen and Sword: On an Arabic Literary Debate", in: *Journal of Semitic Studies* 32 (1987), 329–360, and Wolfhart Heinrichs: "Rose versus narcissus: observations on an Arabic literary debate", in: *Dispute poems and Dialogues in the Ancient and Mediaeval Near East*, ed. G. J. Reinink and H. L. J. Vanstihout (Leuven: Uitgeverij Peeters, 1991), 179–198.

76 See Gelder: "City panegyric, in classical Arabic", in: *Encyclopaedia of Islam*, and *idem.*: "Kufa vs Basra: the literary debate", in: *Asiatische Studien* 50 (1996), 339–362, here 339–341. For the long tradition of literary debates between Mecca and Medina, see e.g. ʿAlī b. Yūsuf az-Zirindī's (d. 772/1370): *al-Munāẓara bayna Makka wa-l-Madīna*, ed. Saʿīd ʿAbd al-Fattāḥ (al-Qāhira: Dār al-Amīn, 1414/1993); as-Suyūṭī's *al-Ḥuǧaǧ al-mubīna fī t-tafḍīl bayna Makka wa-l-Madīna*, ed. by ʿAbd Allāh Muḥammad ad-Darwīš (Dimašq: al-Yamāma, 1985); or his "Sāǧiʿat al-ḥaram fī l-mufāḫara bayn al-Madīna wa-l-Ḥaram", in: *Šarḥ*

The following *mufāḫara* is a literary debate, and more precisely a poetical contest between Baghdad and Damascus, which is part of an ancient and persistent tradition of rivalry between Syria and Iraq,[77] going back politically to the earlier period of Arab-Islamic history. In contrast to the aforementioned types of city panegyrics of a more or less higher culture (in modernist terms), this *mufāḫara* of the late Mamluk or early Ottoman times presents a rare literary piece of vivid popular culture, undermining the seriousness of the established motifs and city-related topics of *ǧadal*[78].

The *mufāḫara*-poem can be found as part of the second appendix to al-Badrī's (d. 894/1488)[79] work *Nuzhat al-anām fī maḥāsin aš-Šam* in the Staatsbibliothek in Berlin (Sprenger 187).[80] In addition to conventional topics of *faḍā'il*, al-Badrī's text is overwrought with explanations and poems concerning the vegetation of Damascus. The copy is dated 1027/1627 (fols. 1-88a) in the colophon, but later (in 1028/1628) expanded with the first appendix (fols. 88b-91a) ending again with a colophon, where the copyist Muḥammad b. Ismāʿīl aṣ-Ṣafadī writes his name. This part con-

Maqāmāt Ǧalāl ad-Dīn as-Suyūṭī, ed. Samīr Maḥmūd ad-Durūbī (Bayrūt: Muʾassasat ar-Risāla, 1989), 499–553; see also Albert Arazi: "Matériaux pour l'étude du conflit de préséance entre le Mekke et Médine", in: *JSAI* 5 (1984), 177–235 and Wagner: *Die arabische Rangstreitdichtung*, 448–449.

77 For a literary reflection of this rivalry, see, for example, the chapter *Iftiḫār aš-Šāmiyyīn ʿalā l-Baṣriyyīn wa-faḍl al-ḥabla ʿalā n-naḫla*, in Ibn al-Faqīh al-Hamaḏānī's *Muḫtaṣar kitāb al-buldān*, ed. de Goeje (Leiden: Brill 1885), 118–128.

78 See Wagner: "Munāẓara", in: *Encyclopaedia of Islam*, 2nd ed.

79 The author is a Syrian anthologist and poet. His full name is Taqī ad-Dīn Abū t-Tuqā (sometimes Abū l-Baqā) Abū Bakr b. ʿAbdallāh b. Muḥammad al-Badrī (847/1443–897/1488). For his life and writings, see Gelder: "al-Badrī, Abū l-Tuqā", in: *Encyclopaedia of Islam, Three* [online].

80 The manuscript was bought in Mosul in 1855 as written on the front page.

tains some contemporary poetry (including a chronogram of Māmayh/ Māmayya ar-Rūmī)[81] about Damascus and biographical data in prose. As a second appendix, aṣ-Ṣafadī adds without further remarks the city-slam: the *Mufāḫarat ad-Dimašqī wa-l-Baġdādī*. The copy has so far not been considered in any of the published editions.

The author of the *mufāḫara* is only known by his pen name an-Nuwāsī, who according to the poem was a cotton trader. An-Nuwāsī, who might also be known as al-Qaṭṭān, presumably lived in the late Mamluk or early Ottoman period in Syria. In addition to textual indicators, this assumption stems mainly from the fact that the first appendix of the ms. contains biographical entries and poetry predominantly from the Mamluk and Ottoman periods in Syria. Among these are Damascan Ottoman-era poets Māmayh (alt. Māmayya) ar-Rūmī and Darwīš aṭ-Ṭālāwī (d. 1016). A similar selection of poets is also found in Ms. Princeton Yehuda (5864 Y), in which Māmayh and – there – al-Qaṭṭān (the same an-Nuwāsī?) are both cited with *mawwāl* poetry.[82]

Plot composition

Verses	1-4	Introduction, poet joining the rivals
Verses	5-8	Reason for their argument
Verses	9-52	*Mufāḫara* between the Damascene and the Baghdadi

[81] For this poet, see Masarwa: "Performing the Occasion: The Chronograms of Māmayya ar-Rūmī", in: *The Mamluk-Ottoman Transition: Continuity and Change in Egypt and Bilād aš-Šām in the Sixteenth Century*, ed. by Stephan Conermann and Gül Şen (Bonn: Vandenhoeck & Ruprecht, 2016), 177–206.

[82] *Ms. Princeton Yehuda (5864 Y)*, fol. 21 b. – I owe special thanks to Kristina Richardson for this Ms. reference.

Verses	53-58	Concession of the Baghdadi and reconciliation
Verses	59-66	Celebration of the reconciliation, parting
Verses	67-68	Poet reveals his pen name (*maḫlaṣ*): an-Nuwāsī al-Qaṭṭān; exhortation
Verses	69-70	Asking forgiveness, blessings

A poet tells a group of people what happened to him during the course of a day by talking directly to them. The scene is Damascus and this is his story: slightly depressed, he had set off to rid himself of his sorrows. In *ar-Rabwa* he encountered two men who had obviously been arguing. They asked him to judge their argument. The Damascene introduces himself and his friend, a Baghdadi. Next, the reason for their argument is given. The Damascene is still speaking and complains about his friend from Baghdad (always called *Ibn Baġdād*). According to the Damascene, the Baghdadi started it and was responsible for their falling out when he exaggerated by praising his own city and claiming that nowhere there is a city like Baghdad (verse 7).

The city-slam takes place in front of the *ḥākim* (judge) and only ends with the Damascene winning when the Baghdadi comes to recognize that he is mistaken. Subsequently they reconcile.[83] It is not so much a compelling virtue of the city as such but a moral argument that causes the Baghdadi to concede: the location of the argument is Damascus, and the Baghdadi is an exile who had sought refuge in Damascus. When the Baghdadi complains that the Damascenes do not know what friendship is (verse 46), the Damascene points out that the Baghdadi, as an expelled person (*yā manfī*

83 The poet in his function as judge is only addressed after the Baghdadi has already surrendered. Up to verse 55 the judge has no particular function and he does not have to pass judgement. Only after the reconciliation of the two opponents does the 'narrator/judge' become active.

min al-mašriq, verse 19) once looked for protection in Damascus (verses 48 and 51). In addition, he points out that the two of them are friends. The Baghdadi thus has to recognize that his accusations are untenable (verses 53-56).

Upon their reconciliation (verses 57-58), the judge invites both of them to an-Nayrab (verses 59-62). The frivolous part starts here and they spend the night partying. After they have gone their separate ways (verse 66), the poet reveals his identity in the *maḫlaṣ* (verse 67); he is an *adīb*, called an-Nuwāsī and a cotton (*qaṭṭān*) trader. Next, he addresses the audience/ readers beseeching them to ignore whoever disparages his poetry and wishing that his detractors go away. The poet asks for forgiveness and God's protection ending his poem by praising and wishing blessings upon the prophet.

Rhyme pattern and compositional features

The poem, an extraordinarily long *mawāliyā* in a recognizable *basīṭ* meter, consists of 35 stanzas, i.e. 70 verses in total. Every stanza has its distinctive monorhyme pattern with two rhyming couplets sharing the same rhyme (*aAaA, bBbB, cCcC* etc., more correctly aaaa, bbbb, cccc etc., as the hemistichs are designated as lines) and corresponding to the *rubāʿī* type of early narrative *mawāliyās*.[84] The stanzas as cohesive units are cleverly

---

[84] Cachia: "mawāliyā", in: *Encyclopaedia of Islam*, 2nd ed., 6: 867–868 and his entry "mawāliyā", in: *Encyclopedia of Arabic Literature*, ed. Julie Scott Meisami and Paul Starkey (London: Routledge, 1998), 2: 518–519. See also, Margaret Larkin: "Popular poetry in the post-classical period", in: *Arabic Literature in the Post-Classical Period*, ed. Roger Allan and D. S. Richards (Cambridge: Cambridge University Press, 2006), esp. 208–212 and Wilhelm Hoenerbach: *Die vulgärarabische Poetik al-Kitāb al-ʿāṭil al-ḥālī wal-muraḫḫaṣ al-ġālī des Ṣafiyyaddīn Ḥillī*, kritisch hrsg. und erklärt von Wilhelm Hoenerbach (Wiesbaden Steiner, 1956), esp. 23–46, 69–72.

composed and display a highly rhythmic pattern. In the debate (*faḫr*) section the poet allows each of the rivals 11 four-line verses each for their performance. But at least one of the four lines/hemistichs is reserved for the poet, introducing the actual speaker and his mood, sometimes stretched into the second line/hemistich, in which case only two lines are left for the performance of the debaters:

first hemistich / line	**rhyme**	**second hemistich / line**	**rhyme**
qāla (*ad-Dimašqī / al-Baġdādī*) + mood	(c)	+ mood or argument verse in direct speech	(c)
argument verse in direct speech / *faḫr* / invective	(c)	argument verse in direct speech / *faḫr* / invective	(c)

From the many styles of the *mufāḫara*, this is a contest between two rivals representing their cities, and not the cities speaking for themselves – which however, does not comply with the definition of the *munāẓara* in the strict sense.[85] The role of the poet is to pretend to offer a formally equal treatment as if the poet were neutral, as he presents himself as an arbitrator who does not intervene, and who moreover is overanxious in his concern with the reconciliation of the opponents (verse 61). The poet allows the Baghdadi to begin but presents his manner of speaking as more cheeky; the Damascene seems to fall behind. But the poet does so, only to offer some suspense when the Damascene reaffirms his superiority against the Baghdadi.

85 See p. 56 in this study.

The language of the *mufāḫara* is colloquial middle Arabic.[86] Presumably both men speak Damascene (as can be assumed from the vernacular style). In this manner, the poet adds another subtle argument for the Syrian side throughout the *mufāḫara*. The poem in the manuscript is rarely vocalized, the *hamza* never occurs, the *tā' marbūṭa* appears as (ه), occasionally the *alif mamdūda* appears instead of the *alif maqṣūra*, casually dotted (ي), while some letters like *ḏ, ǧ, ġ* and *t* are undotted. Some irregularities in the meter occur, which may, however, more often be a result of miswriting or a faulty manuscript. Although the desinential inflection (*i'rāb*) should be avoided in *mawāliyā*, the poet regularly mixes inflected and vernacular forms to fit into the metrical pattern.

The presented arguments of the opponents are rather bold and simple. To display rhetorical skill in the debate (Arabic: *ǧadal)*, which is normally the goal of this genre, was definitely not intended. The Baghdadi, for example, does not offer much more than that Baghdad, the city of the Caliphs, scholars and ascetics (verse 41), is situated on the banks of the Tigris (verse 33) and he merely enumerates these facts. Not knowing his own city's illustrious past and the long tradition of Baghdad's city panegyrics reflects badly on the Baghdadi somehow. Rarely do the two rivals react to the preceding argument. Instead, they mainly react with emotional and moral phrases like: *listen! don't exaggerate! what are you talking about? And you are only a puffer!* etc. followed by an enumeration of their own beauties and merits. With the exception of verses 45-46, the rebuke they offer does not consist of anything more.

The organization of the poem's narrated timeline shows inconsistencies between the narrator time and the plot time: the poet begins by saying 'what happened to me today'. According to the Arabic/Islamic tradition,

86 E.g., verses 20, 21, 32 and 35.

the day starts in the evening before, and even considering this convention, the time covered in this poem seems to be longer than just a day. The narration starts in the daytime, carries on beyond the night until the next morning, when then, at the earliest, the narrator could have told the audience his story. Apart from this, the poet breaks the tension when the rivals reconcile (verses 53–58), however, this might also be the fault of missing verses in the manuscript.

The poet also omits any artful allusion to literary traditions in city panegyrics. Taking a closer look at the modes of giving praise, we can observe that at first they consist mainly of lauding the beauty of the opponents' bodies (respectively their city) employing conventional comparisons to face, cheeks, eyes, hair, legs, posterior, hips, breath, mouth and breasts. Most of the arguments are self-advertising instead of praising the city:

12 *"Don't you see the flowers and apples on my cheeks (my flowerlike and apple-like cheeks)? / And the lance of my stature and the twig/branch of my figure?"*

14 *"Look at my forehead and my connected eyebrows! / And I have a charming figure, how many are addicted to it!"*

15 *"The Damascene said: "The blackness of the night came from my hair / and the musk from my breath and the pearls from my mouth."*

26 *"Exalted beauty is my fate, for God the exalted is my creator. / Part of the perfection of my splendor is my good character."*

The city is beautiful because of the speakers' own attractiveness, who display features of female beauty – corresponding to the gender of cities in Arabic – regardless of the fact that they are men.

Indeed, after a first read one might wonder to what extent the poet contributes to the genre of panegyrics. To break out into invectives or by reiterating serial sets of canonized motifs of praise could not have been the greatest challenge. Even in the invective part the poet hardly makes any effort to present a counter-concept for what he is criticizing. But read as a parody or a playful reverberation of "classical" models this text reveals its cunning effects with all the disruptions of formal and aesthetic and even intellectual demands of the genre. The fact that the poet explicitly addresses his first verse to *al-qudwa* (paragon of more elaborate *mufāḫaras*) while using the poetic form of a semi-colloquial *mawāliyā*, his audacious and contemptuous remarks in the *maḫlaṣ*, and perhaps his name an-Nuwāsī (allusion to Abū Nuwās) are further evidence of this being a parody intended for a popular/common audience, – well suited for a performance on stage or in a coffeehouse. The poet seems to subvert the *mufāḫara* by consciously violating the specifics of the genre and the norms of more elaborate pieces.

Exceeding and playing with the genre forms was one of the features of parody. This *mufāḫara* is presented as a playful parody of city panegyrics, which in Mikhail Bakhtin's terms is a kind of carnivalized literature, mocking canonized forms and expressions, where the world is "*turned upside-down, ideas and truths are endlessly tested and contested, and thus de-privileged*."[87] According to Bakhtin and Yury Tynyanov, a parody can

---

87 *The Routledge Dictionary of Literary Terms*, ed. Peter Child and Roger Fowler (London: Routledge, 2006), 53. According to Bakhtin, the "logic of carnivals is essentially the logic of reversals, of the world upside down, of burlesque coronations and dethronings, and of the substitution of high for low and faces for bottoms and vice versa" (cited in Eleazar Moiseevich Meletinskiĭ: *The Poetics of Myth*, transl. by Guy Lanoue and Alexandre Sadetsky (London: Routledge, 2000), 112).

be seen as a kind of safety valve to help maintain social equilibrium.[88] One cannot understand parody without reference to the parodied material/ form, as it exceeds the boundaries of the given canonized text and their devices through imitation and recreation concomitantly.[89]

Accordingly, this *mawāliyā-mufāḫara* is not devoid of innovative elements concerning both form and content, for it displays an inversion of all the features mentioned concerning the personification of cities. We saw in some previous examples, how the use of the rhetorical figure of *tašbīh* (simile) had the effect of humanizing the city, while to a certain extent simultaneously dehumanizing the person. We then also had examples of a metonymical or more causal relationship between city and inhabitants where the city leaves an imprint on the human sphere (habits, mentalities etc.) – and, as shown in the case of the city-slam, vice versa.

After much effort had been put into the personification of the city in classical times, in this case the person becomes the city as the man has urbanized or citified himself. The rivals leave the relevant topic behind – the topic almost becomes trans-urban. The cities do not speak for themselves as cities, moreover we observe a reversal of a personification, as in the case of a reverse simile (*at-tašbīh al-maqlūb*).

---

88 Margaret A. Rose: *Parody: Ancient, Modern and Post-modern* (Cambridge: University Press, 2000), 147, see also Meletinskiĭ: *The Poetics of Myth*, 112.

89 For Tynyanov, see Jurij Striedter (ed.): *Russischer Formalismus. Texte zur allgemeinen Literaturtheorie und zur Theorie der Prosa* (München: Fink Verlag, 1994), 302–371, esp. 331 and Rose: *Parody: Ancient, Modern and Post-modern*, 117 ff.

Regardless of whether this poem was written by a less talented poet – for which there is of course evidence[90] – or not, we certainly gain knowledge about the versatility of the *mufāḫara* genre and how varied the options were for toying with this genre's conventions. In both cases, in its classical usage and also in this parodic usage, the *mufāḫara* remains a highly important social institution.[91] It is possible to raise the question whether this was a sediment of a higher literary culture of Ottoman-Damascene society in the 15th century, some kind of light literature, which offers further insight into the question of which circles adapted and diversified which kind of literature. Moreover, it shows which media existed and which strategies could be employed to display urban consciousness and perform urbanity.

90 See p. 63 in this study.

91 See Wagner: "Mufākhara, [1]", in: *Encyclopaedia of Islam*, 2nd ed., 7: 308–309.

Conclusion

This study outlined and discussed some examples of city panegyrics in different genres of texts, be they religious, secular or hybrid. It was stressed that these genres should not be considered simply as forms of paradigmatic adulation (in the case of poetry), because of their classical patterns or hagiography (in the case of prose), because they were presenting religious evidence.

What does the praise of a city in literature say about the real city? In his famous work *Art as technique* (1917) the Russian Formalist Viktor Šklovskij (d. 1984) concludes his discussion of the term defamiliarization: "*The purpose of art is to impart the sensation of things as they are perceived and not as they are known.*"[92] Accordingly, the city offers a space for experiencing life, while the city-panegyric offers a new space for experiencing life, namely within the 'space of the arts'. The emphasis on rhetorical devices and the patterns in and behind them indicate the individual as well as the perception of collective space, the awareness of urbanity and the urban ideals as perceived by the agents communicating them. None of these perceptions were stable, as they were always contested, denied, or reaffirmed. A closer reading of literary city imagery enhances our ability to connect them with the historical reality/(-ies) of cities.

Dealing with aesthetic and highly stylized texts, some substantial data will get lost if they are read primarily and solely according to the question

92 Viktor Šklovskij's "Art as Technique", in: *Russian Formalist Criticism: Four Essays*, ed. Lee T. Lemon and Marion J. Reis (Lincoln: Univ. of Nebraska Press, 1965), 12.

of the apparent spatial paradigm and the events of reality. As Šklovskij expands in his discussion of poetic imagery:

> *An image is not a permanent referent for those mutable complexities of life which are revealed through it; its purpose is not to make us perceive meaning, but to create a special perception of the object – it creates a 'vision' of the object instead of serving as a means for knowing it.*[93]

The panegyric of cities as a rhetorical amplifier and as an exaggerated hymn of the 'real' city shows the tension between textual and urban realities. Urban space in texts requires a differentiated analysis of motifs of praise and criticism. The functions of such devices have to be analyzed inter- and intra-textually. As the examples have demonstrated, praise and criticism of a city encapsulate a counterproposal for the perception and vision of the city. This embedded counterproposal can be unearthed by detecting and inverting the rhetorical devices and figures.

93 Viktor Šklovskij: "Art as Technique", 18.

Appendix

Downfall of a minaret in the year 762/1361

In: al-Maqrīzī, Aḥmad Ibn ʿAlī: *al-Mawāʿiẓ wa-l-Iʿtibār fī Ḏikr al-Ḫiṭaṭ wa-l-Āṯār* (Bulāq: 1853), 2: 316.

1 أَبْشِرْ فَسَعْدُكَ يَا سُلْطَانَ مِصْرَ أَتَى   بَشِيرُهُ بِمَقَالٍ سَارَ كَالْمَثَلِ

2 إِنَّ الْمَنَارَةَ لَمْ تَسْقُطْ لِمَنْقَصَةٍ   لَكِنْ لِسِرٍّ خَفِيٍّ قَدْ تَبَيَّنَ لِي

3 مِنْ تَحْتِهَا قُرِئَ الْقُرْآنُ فَاسْتَمَعَتْ   فَالْوَجْدُ فِي الْحَالِ أَدَّاهَا إِلَى الْمَيْلِ

4 لَوْ أَنْزَلَ اللهُ قُرْآنًا عَلَى جَبَلٍ   تَصَدَّعَتْ رَأْسُهُ مِنْ شِدَّةِ الْوَجَلِ

5 تِلْكَ الْحِجَارَةُ لَمْ تَنْقَضَّ بَلْ هَبَطَتْ   مِنْ خَشْيَةِ اللهِ لَا لِلضَّعْفِ وَالْخَلَلِ

6 وَغَابَ سُلْطَانُهَا فَاسْتَوْحَشَتْ وَرَمَتْ   بِنَفْسِهَا لِجَوًى فِي الْقَلْبِ مُشْتَعِلِ

7 فَالْحَمْدُ لِلهِ حَظُّ الْعَيْنِ زَالَ بِمَا   قَدْ كَانَ قَدَّرَهُ الرَّحْمَنُ فِي الْأَزَلِ

8 لَا يَعْتَرِي الْبُؤْسُ بَعْدَ الْيَوْمِ مَدْرَسَةً   شُيِّدَتْ بُنْيَانُهَا بِالْعِلْمِ وَالْعَمَلِ

9 وَدُمْتَ حَتَّى تَرَى الدُّنْيَا بِهَا امْتَلَأَتْ   عِلْمًا فَلَيْسَ بِمِصْرَ غَيْرُ مُشْتَغِلِ

Edition: Mufāḫarat ad-Dimašqī wa-l-Baġdādī

In: Ms. Sprenger 187, fols. 92a-93b.

مفاخرة الدمشقي والبغدادي

بسم الله الرحمن الرحيم

I

1 قِفْ واسْتمِعْ يا أَيها القدوهْ   ما تمَّ لي اليوم معْ إثنينِ في الرَّبوهْ
2 خرجتُ أَمشي لأَرمي الهمَّ في النَّدوهْ   لقيتُ إثنينِ عبّوا المقلْ في خلوهْ

II

3 لما رأوني بقى الاثنينِ يَا حضَّار   يسْموا إليّ وواحدْهمْ إليّ شارْ
4 وقالَ اجلسْ وأحكمْ بيننا يا جارْ   جارَ الرِّضا أنت والمقبولُ منّكْ صَارْ

III

5 أَنا دمشقِي وهذا الشَّخصُ بغدادي   قمنا طَلعْنا وزادهْ حطَّ مع زاديْ
6 لمّا جلسنا وطبنا جنبَ ذا الوادي   بدا تكلَّمْ وكان الذَّنبُ لِلبَادِيْ

IV

7 وقال مثلُ بلادي ليس يوجدْ قطّْ   بحفِّها ثمَّ دجلتْها وما الشَّطّْ
8 وقد رفَعْ مجدَ بَلْدَتْهمْ وحلّقْ حطّ   لا شكَّ إنه تعدَّى وَاعْتدى وَاشْتَطّْ

V

9	قال ابنُ بغدادَ سِيدي ليسَ في الآفاقْ	كمثلِ بغدادَ بلْدةْ نزهةِ العُشَّاقْ
10	وأنا جبيني يضي كالشَّمسِ في الإشراقْ	ولي عيونٌ قواتلْ نبلُهمْ رشَّاقْ

VI

11	قال الدّمشقِي وخدُّهْ بالعرَقْ ندي	لا شكَّ أنَّكْ بهذا القول متعدي
12	أمَا ترى الوردَ والتّفّاحَ من خدّي	والرُّمحَ من قامتي والغصنَ من قدّي

VII

13	قال ابن بغداد وهو مما قد سَمِعْ مغبونْ	لا شكَّ أنّكْ مقرقِعْ يَا صبي مجنونْ
14	أما ترى جبهتي مع حَاجِبِي المقرونْ	ولي قوامٌ مهفهفْ كم به مفتونْ

VIII

15	قال الدّمشقِي سواد اللّيلِ من شعري	والمسكُ من نكهتي والدُّرّ من ثغري
16	ولي نهودٌ حكتْ رمّان في صدري	ومثل طيّ النّطَاقِي ينطوي خصري

IX

17	قال ابْنُ بغدادَ اسمَعْ يا صبِي وصفِي	قد حزتُ كلَّ البها والحسن والظَّرْفِي
18	ولي جبين ضِيَاهُ للقمرْ يخفي	قدِّي ونهدِي ولا تنس الذي خَلْفِي

X

19	قال الدّمشقِي وَهو ممَّا قَدْ سَمِعْ مطرقْ	قد زدتَ في الوصف يا منفي مِنَ المشرقْ

20 أَما ترى وجنتي كالشَّمسِ إذ تشْرق   ولي عيونٌ قواتلْ للزَّرد تخْرِق

XI

21 قال ابن بغداد أيشْ ذا القولُ يا ابن الشامْ   هلْ أنت نائمْ والاَّ انتَ في الأحلامْ

22 أليس تَعْلَمْ بأني جيتُ من أقوامْ   ما يرتضوكَ تكنْ من جملة الخدّامْ

XII

23 قال الدّمشقي وخدّه مثلُ لون الوردْ   يا من علينا فَشرْ إسمعْ كلام الجدْ

24 أما ترى طولَ شعري واعتدالَ القدّ   وأنت ما أرتضي أنَّكْ تكون لي عبدْ

XIII

25 قال ابن بغداد ما تنظرْ إلى ساقِي   أبيضْ سقيل وكلُّ النّاسِ عشّاقي

26 والحسنُ قسمي تعالى الله خلاّقي   ومن تمامِ بهائي طيبُ أخلاقي

XIV

27 قال الدّمشقي تمام الحسن هوْ منّي   وأنتَ فشّار يا هذا وفي ظنّي

28 بأنّ ردَّ جوابكْ ضائعٌ مني   قلْ لي بأيّ الخصائلْ تفتخرْعنّي

XV

29 قال ابنُ بغداد انا ابنُ الكَرَمْ والجودْ   وجودنا لمْ يزل بين الورى موجودْ

30 وفي السّخا والعطايا نبذَل المجهودْ   وعندنا الشّطُّ نزهة خلقة المعبودْ

XVI

31 قال الدّمشقِي تَأَدّب لا تكن فشّارْ   دمشقُ ما مثلها في سائرَ الأقطارْ

32 ستّ البلادْ بِالجوامعْ خَصّها الجبّارْ   بالجامِع الأموي والسّبعَة الأنْهارْ

XVII

33 قال ابنُ بغدادَ نحنا عندنا أشرحْ   دجلةْ مليحةْ وماها لَمْ يزلْ يمرحْ

34 أمّا الملاحُ عليها لم تزل تمرحْ   شبه الطّواويسِ في غيضانها تمرحْ

XVIII

35 قال الدّمشقِي ونحنا عندنا ميدانْ   وقصرُ أبلقْ مثاله ما رأى إنسانْ

36 أمّا المروجُ كثيرَةْ بأرضنا ألوانْ   بها الملاحُ عليها كُنّهم غزلانْ

XIX

37 قال ابنُ بغدادَ كم في أرضنا بستانْ   حدائقُهْ باسِقةْ إثمارها ألوانْ

38 ولو رأيت الجزاير كنّها يا إنسانْ   جَنّةْ وأهل الجزايرْ كنَّهم ولدانْ

XX

39 قال الدّمشقِي ونحنا عندنا فرجاتْ   جبهة وربوة ثمّ ورديّاتْ

40 [و] امّا جباب البنفسجْ نزهة النّزهاتْ   والصّالحيّةْ تعشّقْ بالخميسيات

XXI

41 قال ابن بغدادَ لو تنظرْ إلى بغدادْ   مدينة الخلفا والعلمِ والزّهّادْ

42 مدينةٌ أهلها أهل الذّكا أجوادْ   وكم بها عالمٌ في علمهِ قد سادْ

XXII

43 قال الدّمشقِي بلادي فضلُها مشهورْ   كم من نبيّ ترى في أرضها مقبورْ

44 دِمشقَ دامَ عليها البها والنورْ   وأهلها في بهاهمْ يشبهون الحورْ

XXIII

45 قال ابن بغداد يا شامي هواكُمْ سمّْ   وماؤكُمْ ينقلوا عنه بأنه دمْ

46 وقطّ صاحب صحبته يا فتى ما تمّْ   هَذِي ثَلاثُ خِصَالٍ فِيكُمُ تُذَمّْ

XXIV

47 قال الدّمشقِي وَهُوْ قد اعتبنْ واحْدق   قديت قلبِي بقولكْ يا قَوافي قدّْ

48 نحنا نقيمُ على الصّحبةْ ونرعى الوِدّْ   وليسَ من طَبْعَنا للجيدِ ننقضْ عهدْ

XXV

49 قال ابن بغداد كَمْ ذا يا صبِي تشتطْ   ميّزْ كلامكْ ولا تسفهْ علينا قطْ

50 الدّهرُ يقبضْ على الإنسانِ بعد البسطْ   ما [أ]نا حقيرٌ ولا قدري بقى مُنْحطْ

XXVI

51 قال الدّمشقِي ونحنا اجدادنا أخيَارْ   ووالدي كَم بجاههْ مُلتجي قد جارْ

52 نحنا نقيمُ على الصّحبةْ ونرعى الجارْ   ولا نجورُ عليه إن سطا أو جارْ

XXVII

53 قام ابن بغداد استغفر وصلحه مال   وقد خضع وتذلّلْ غاية الإذلالْ

54 وقالَ يا اهلَ السّخا والجودِ والإفضالْ   ومثلُ جلّقْ مدينةْ ما خَطَرْ بالبالْ

XXVIII

55 وقالَ لي يا أديبْ اشهدْ على لفظي — بأنّ هذا الدّمشقِي هو الذي مَحْظي
56 وأنّ أهلهْ وأرضهْ خير من أرضي — وانا عبيدٌ لَهُ بالرّوحْ له أرضي

XXIX

57 لمّا سمعْ قولهُ الشّامي نهَضْ سرعهْ — وقد تبسّمْ بوجْهْ أبهى مِنَ الشّمعَهْ
58 سما إليه وبادرْ قبّلهْ سبعهْ — وصالحوا وارتصوا فِي ذَلِكَ البُقْعَهْ

XXX

59 لمّا بدا الصّلحُ فيما بينهم ناديتْ — اثنينهم بلطافةْ والكلامْ ألقيتْ
60 قالوا مرادُكَ قلتوا شرّفوا للبيتْ — قاموا وقمتُ أنا قدّامُهمْ مدّيتْ

XXXI

61 بقيتُ أمشي وهمْ يا اهلَ الذّكا والفهمْ — يمشونَ خلفي وقلبي ما خلا منْ وهمْ
62 حتّى أتينا إلى النّيربْ وأرض السّهمْ — جينا الصّواحْ وعنّي زال كلّ الهمّْ

XXXII

63 جيتوا إلى البيت افتحْ قلتُ يا فتّاحْ — من غيبِه الرزقُ من فضلِهْ بلا مفتاحْ
64 فتحت جاز الدّمشقِي كالقَمَرْ إذ لاحْ — وإبنُ بغدادَ بعْدُهْ جدّد الأفراحْ

XXXIII

65 بتنا بليلةْ هنيةْ طيّبةْ يا قومْ — نلعبْ ونضحكْ وما فيها أخذنا نومْ
66 لمّا اقبل الحبُّ أقضينا تمام اليومْ — وفارقوني وخلّوا دمْعَ عيني عومْ

XXXIV

67 وانا الأديب النّواسِي صنْعتِي قطّانْ   غلامُ أهل الذّكا والسّادَة الفطّان

68 قلْ للّذي عابِ نظمي لا تكنْ غلطانْ   يفشرْ ويخسا ويتْلطّى مع الحيطانْ

XXXV

69 واستغفر الله من ذا القولِ يا حضّار   ومن ذنوبي وزلاّتي مع الأوزارْ

70 ثمّ الصَّلاةُ على خيْرِ الورا المختارْ   محمّد المصطفى في السّرِّ والإِجهارْ

Translation

I 1 Halt! And listen, oh (great) paragon,[94] / what happened to me and two people in ar-Rabwa today.

2 I moved out to relieve myself from sorrow, / and met two men secludedly in a corner.

II 3 As they saw me, my dear audience, / they called me, and one of them was pointing at me.

4 He said: "Sit down and judge between us, neighbor. / A pleasant companion you are to us, and whatever you decide, your verdict will be accepted."[95]

III 5 I am a Damascene and this one is a Baghdadi. / We set out and ventured forth and shared our provisions.[96]

6 We sat down and enjoyed ourselves in the valley / he started to speak – the fault lies with the one who starts to argue.

IV 7 He said: "Nowhere is there a city like mine with her riverbanks,[97] there is her Tigris and the waters of aš-Šaṭṭ."

---

94 The meter is defective and does not scan; the second foot (– ∪ –) of the first line is missing.

95 Read *maqbūl*, instead of *qubūl* of the ms.

96 Read *zādah*, instead of *zādahu*.

97 The ms. has *ḥaffīha*, which could be a miswriting of *ḥusnihā* (her beauty).

8 Thus, he elevated the glory of his city, / undoubtedly going too far."[98]

V 9 The Baghdadi said: "Dear Sir! There is nothing in the whole world / that compares to Baghdad. A city like a place of joy for lovers.

10 Lo and behold! My forehead, it gleams like the sun at sunrise. / I have killing eyes, whose arrows are true to their aim.

VI 11 The Damascene said, while his cheeks were moistened by sweat: "No doubt! You exaggerated vastly (you are hostile) in your speech.[99]

12 Don't you see the flowers and apples on my cheeks (my flowerlike and apple-like cheeks)? / And the lance of my stature and the twig/branch of my figure?" (more literally: The lance's stature was inspired by my physique and the branch was inspired by my shape.")

VII 13 The Baghdadi said, and he felt himself falling behind by what he had heard:[100] / "No doubt that you are just jabbering (making noise), you madman!

---

98 Read colloquial *innū*, instead of *innahū*.

99 Read perhaps *muʿtadī* (encroaching, hostile) for *mutaʿaddī* (transgressing, unjust, tyrant, encroaching). Read in either way, the last two feet do not scan properly.

100 The third foot seems to be too long; the line does scan if *qad* is omitted and read *wahwam-ma samiʿ maġbūn*.

14 Look at my forehead and my connected eyebrows! / And I have a charming figure, how many are addicted to it!"

VIII 15 The Damascene said: "The blackness of the night came from my hair / and the musk from my breath and the pearls from my mouth.

16 I have breasts that resemble pomegranates / and like with a belt my waist is folded up."[101]

IX 17 The Baghdadi said: "Now listen to my description! I have collected all the splendor, beauty, and elegance.

18 My forehead's glimmer surpasses the moon. (Look) at my stature, my breasts and don't forget what is behind me (my rear)."[102]

X 19 The Damascene said, embarrassed about what he had heard:[103] / "Now you have massively exaggerated with your description, you who are expelled from the East.

20 Look at my cheeks, like the rising sun. / My killing eyes (glances) pierce all coats of mail."[104]

---

101 The ms. has something like التطاق, النطاق, however *niṭāq* without the article makes more sense in this context.

102 The ms. has the colloquial لا تنسي.

103 The line only scans when *qad* is omitted and the pronoun is read *wa-hū*.

104 The ms. has *li-z-zarad* but perphaps *li-z-zurūd* is more plausible. The line scans if read *wa-lī ʿuyūnun qawātil li-z-zarad (-zurūd) taḫriq*.

XI 21 The Baghdadi said: "What are you talking about, you Šāmī? / Are you asleep, or are you dreaming?[105]

22 Don't you know that I come from a people / who would not even accept you as a servant?"

XII 23 The Damascene said, with reddened cheeks: "You, who you boast in front of us! Better listen now to my serious words!"

24 Behold the splendor of my hair's length and the straightness of my stature. / And you, you would not suffice if you were my slave!"

XIII 25 The Baghdadi said: "Don't you see my calves, like a polished blade[106] for which all men have fallen.[107]

26 Exalted beauty is my fate, for God the exalted is my creator. / Part of the perfection of my splendor is my good character."[108]

---

105 Read perhaps [...] *wa-allā anta fī-l-aḥlām*; the more proper (collq.) *willā nta* does not scan.

106 Read *saqīl* with nunation, otherwise the line does not scan properly.

107 Lit.: "all are in love with me."

108 Also possible: "From the perfection of my elegance comes the goodness of my good behavior."

XIV 27 The Damascene said: "The perfection of beauty, it is mine! / And you are only a puffer![109] In my view,

28 you are not even worthy of a reply! / Tell me, of what kind of achievement[110] will you boast in front of me?"

XV 29 The Baghdadi said: "I am the son of the generous and the munificent (the real x-one is me). / Our generosity is well known."

30 We do our best in regard to largess and generosity. / We have aš-Šaṭṭ as an attraction created by the most adored."

XVI 31 The Damascene said, "Behave and don't be outrageous! / A place that resembles Damascus is nowhere to be found.

32 She is the princess of cities. God has equipped her with / mosques, with the Umayyad Mosque and the seven rivers."

XVII 33 The Baghdadi said: "And we, in our city the beautiful Tigris flows. / Its waters flow tranquilly.

34 And beautiful women stroll on its banks, / resembling peacocks on its meadows."

---

109 Neither *fušār* "idle talk" nor *faššār* "swaggerer" scan properly in the second foot of the second line.

110 The ms. has *ḥaṣāʾil*, one might also read *ḫaṣāʾil* (sg. *ḫaṣīla*, quality).

XVIII 35 The Damascene said: "And we, we have the Maydān, / and the Ablaq palace. Mankind has not seen their like![111]

36 Lush meadows of all kind we have! / There are such beauties as if they were gazelles."[112]

XIX 37 The Baghdadi said: "How many gardens our country has, / orchards with magnificent trees that bear fruits of all kinds.[113]

38 And if you had seen the Ǧazīra! Man! / She is like a paradise and her inhabitants are like the boys of paradise."[114]

XX 39 The Damascene said: "We, we have the attractions / of Ǧabha and Rabwa [...][115] then also the Wardiyyāt.

40 (Don't forget) Remember Ǧibāb al-Banafsaǧ is the utmost goal of refreshing getaways[116] / and aṣ-Ṣāliḥiyya is ardently desired on Thursdays."

---

111 The ms. has راءٓ for رأى. The meter requires the colloquial reading *miṯālū* for *miṯāluhū*.

112 The ms. has vocalized *kunnahum* for classical *ka-annahum*.

113 The meter requires *ḥadā'iqū* for *ḥadā'iquhū*.

114 *Kunnahā* of the first line is followed by an overlong foot, which does not scan properly. Read *kunnahā yā n-sān* for *ka-innahā yā insān*.

115 The second line does not scan properly. There seems to be a word missing after *Rabwa*.

116 The line only scans if *wa* is omitted.

XXI 41 The Baghdadi said: "If you see Baghdad, / she is the city of the caliphs, of knowledge and ascetics.[117]

42 A city whose inhabitants are wise and magnanimous residents. / And how many a scholar (is) there in high charge by his knowledge."

XXII 43 The Damascene said: "The merits of my city are well known. / (Do you know,) how many prophets are buried on her ground?

44 Damascus, may her splendor and light last forever![118] Her inhabitants resemble the dark-eyed damsels of Paradise in their splendor."

XXIII 45 The Baghdadi said to the Damascene: "Your air is poison / and it is said of your waters that they are blood.[119]

46 The supposed friend never remains a friend, oh brave little man! / Those three characteristics of yours need to be blamed."

XXIV 47 The Damascene felt being harmed and cornered and said: / "You tore my heart asunder with these words, mean rhymester!

---

117 Read *madīnati l-ḫulafā wa-l-ʿilmi* for *madīnati l-ḫulafāʾi wa-l-ʿilmi*.

118 There might be a long syllable missing, however, the line reads: *ʿalayhā l-bahā wa-n-nūr* instead of: *ʿalayhā l-bahāʾ wa-n-nūr*.

119 Read *bi-annū dam* instead of *bi-annahū dam*.

48 We do indeed care for friendship and value affection. / And it is not in our nature to shun our obligations to a good man."

XXV 49 The Baghdadi said: "How often have you digressed now, boy! / Be careful with your words and don't be impertinent towards us.

50 Sooner or later fate strikes back after a period of luck. / I am neither contemptuous nor was my rank ever put down!"[120]

XXVI 51 The Damascene said: "Our ancestors are outstanding personalities.[121] / And my father, how many people seeking refuge, were saved by his wealth.

52 We do care for friendship and respect our neighbor. / And we do not treat him unfairly even if he has attacked us or has erred."

XXVII 53 The Baghdadi stood up and asked for God's forgiveness and bowed down conciliatorily. / He was defeated and was extremely humble."

---

120 The second line does not scan in the first foot; perhaps *mā* and *anā* were read together. The ms. indicates this also, where the *alif* is written afterwards under the line.

121 Read *wa-naḥnā ǧdādunā*.

54 And he said: "You magnanimous people, you brave and chosen![122] / I can't think of another city like Ǧilliq".[123]

XXVIII 55 Then he (the Baghdadi) said to me: "You *adīb*, be my witness for this, my statement, / that the Damascene is the lucky one.[124]

56 And that his people and his country are better than my country, / and I am prepared to serve as a slave with my soul."[125]

XXIX 57 When the Syrian heard his words, he stood up quickly / and smiled happily at him with a face shining brighter than a candle.

58 He got up and went to him to kiss him seven times.[126] / They reconciled and agreed upon this on this place.

XXX 59 After the reconciliation became obvious I called / them with friendliness and words.[127]

---

122 The first line only scans if it is read: *wa-qāla yā-hla s-saḫā* [for *saḫāʾi*] *wa-l-ǧūdi wa-l-ifḍāl*.

123 The ms. has *ḥ-l-q* for *ǧ-l-q*.

124 The ms. has *m-ḫ-ṭ* for *m-ḥ-ẓ*.

125 The last feet in the first line are probably read: *ḫayra min arḍī*. In the second line *wa-anā* is reduced to *wā-nā*.

126 The first line scans when read: *qabbalū sabʿa*.

127 The ms. has *alġayt* for *alqayt*.

60 They said: "What is your wish?" I said to them: "Come along with me to the house".[128] / They got up and I got up as well. I went ahead.

XXXI 61 While I was going farther and they, O people of intellect and insight, / they went behind me, my heart was not really freed of doubt.

62 Only when we reached an-Nayrab and the place as-Sahm, / and we came to the right people, I was liberated from sorrow.

XXXII 63 I came to the house: "Open the door, you Opener", I said, / "the one who provides for men despite his absence; the one whose grace exists without a key."

64 I opened (the door), the Damascene entered like the moon, which rises, / and the Baghdadi followed him, renewing the celebration of joy.

XXXIII 65 We spent the night pleasantly and happily, my people, / we played and laughed and there was no sleeping.

66 When the friends came,[129] we completed the day / and when they left me, they caused my eyes to tear up.

---

128 Read either *murādak [fa-] qultū* (for *qultu) šarrifū* or *murāduka qultū šarrifū*.

129 The first foot only scans if the *hamza* of *aqbala* is elided and read – contrary to classical grammar – with *waṣla*, i.e. *lammā qbala l-ḥubbu*, whereas in *aqḍayna* it retains.

XXXIV 67 I am the littérateur an-Nuwāsī and my profession is the cotton trade.[130] / I am a servant/menial of the clever people and the lords with sharp intellect.

68 Tell him who blames my poetry, 'do not make a mistake!' He is just jabbering and should get lost! He should clave (his forehead against?) to the wall!" (or: he should shelter himself, creep away to the wall).[131]

XXXV 69 I ask God for forgiveness for these words, my dear audience, / and for my sins, my mistakes and trespasses.

70 Then I ask for blessing and salvation for the best of all creatures, / Mohammed the chosen one of the hidden and revealed world.

---

130 Read the first foot *wā-nāl adībun* for *anā l-adībun*.

131 For the Form I and VIII of لطأ and لطى: to shelter, to clave, stick, to beat, crush, and VI: *talaṭṭā ʿalā*: to shelter oneself, to lurk for watching (the enemy), see Lane: *Arabic-English Lexicon* (repr. Cambridge 1984), II: v.s. *l-ṭ-ā* and Hava: *Arabic-English Dictionary* (Beirut 1899), v.s. *l-ṭ-y*.

Bibliography

Primary Sources: Manuscripts

Ms. 5864 Y, Princeton Yehuda

Ms. Nuruosmaniye 3802, Süleymaniye Istanbul

Ms. Sprenger 187, Staatsbibliothek zu Berlin

Primary Sources: Edited Works

Abū Šāma, Šihāb ad-Dīn: *Ar-Rawḍatayn fī aḫbār ad-dawlatayn an-nūriyya wa-ṣ-ṣalāḥiyya wa-yalīhi aḏ-ḏayl ʿalā tarāǧim riǧāl al-qarnayn as-sādis wa-s-sābiʿ*, ed. Ibrāhīm Šams ad-Dīn, vol. 5 of 5 (Bayrūt: Dār al-Kutub al-ʿIlmiyya, 1422/2002).

al-Badrī, Taqī ad-Dīn: *Nuzhat al-anām fī maḥāsin aš-Šām*, ed. Ibrāhīm Ṣāliḥ (Damascus: Dār al-Bašāʾir, 2006).

al-Baġdādī, Abū Bakr al-Ḫaṭīb: *Tārīḫ Baġdād*. ed. Baššār ʿAwwād Maʿrūf, 17 vols. (Bayrūt: Dār al-Ġarb al-Islāmī 1422/2001).

al-Ǧāhiẓ, Abū ʿUṯmān ʿAmr: *Rasāʾil*, ed. Muḥammad Hārūn (al-Qāhira: Maktabat al-Ḫānǧī, 1964).

al-Hamaḏānī Ibn al-Faqīh: *Muḫtaṣar kitāb al-buldān*, ed. Michael Jan de Goeje (Leiden: Brill 1885).

Ibn ʿAbd Rabbih, Aḥmad b. Muḥammad: *al-ʿIqd al-farīd,* ed. Mufīd Muḥammad Qumayḥa, 9 vols. (Bayrūt: Dār al-Kutub al-ʿIlmiyya, 1404/1983).

Ibn Baṭṭūṭa: *Riḥlat Ibn Baṭṭūṭa al-musammā: Tuḥfat an-nuẓẓār fī ġarāʾib al-amṣār wa-ʿaǧāʾib al-asfār*, ed. Darwīš al-Ǧuwaydī, 2 vols. in 1. (Bayrūt: al-Maktaba al-ʿAṣriyya, 2004).

Ibn al-Ǧawzī, Abū l-Farāğ: *Manāqib Baġdād*, ed. Muḥammad Bahğat al-Aṯarī. (Baġdād: Maṭba'at Dār as-Salām, 1342 [1923/1924]).

Ibn Ǧubayr: *Riḥlat Ibn Ǧubayr,* ed. Ḫusayn Naṣṣār (al-Qāhira: Maktabat Miṣr, 1992).

Ibn Ǧubayr: *The Travels of Ibn Jubayr: being the chronicle of a Spanish moor concerning his journey to the Egypt of Saladin, the holy cities of Arabia, Baghdad the city of the Caliphs, the Latin kingdom of Jerusalem, and the Norman kingdom of Sicily*, translated by Ronald J. C. Broadhurst (London: Cape, 1952).

Ibn Iyās: *Die Chronik des Ibn Ijās*, ed. Mohamed Mostafa (Stuttgart: Steiner, 1975).

Ibn Iyās: *Nuzhat al-umam fī ʿağāʾib wa-l-ḥikam*, ed. Muḥammad ʿIzb (Cairo: Madbūlī, 1995).

Ibn Nubāta: *Dīwān Ibn Nubātah al-Miṣrī*, ed. al-Qalqīlī (Miṣr [Cairo]: Maṭba'at at-Tamaddun, 1323/1905).

Ibn ar-Rāʿī (Ibn Ḫudāwirdī), Muḥammad: *al-Barq al-mutaʾalliq fī maḥāsin Ǧilliq*, bi-taḥqīq Muḥammad Adīb al-Ǧādir (Dimašq: Maṭbūʿāt Mağmaʿ al-Luġa al-ʿArabiyya bi-Dimašq, 1429/2008).

Ibn Ṣaṣrā: *A Chronicle of Damascus (1389–1397) by Muḥammad ibn Muḥammad ibn Ṣaṣrā. The unique Bodleian Library manuscript of Kitāb ad-Durra al-muḍīʾa fī d-dawla aẓ-ẓāhiriyya,* translated, ed. and annotated by William M. Brinner, 2 vols. (Berkeley and Los Angeles: University of California Press, 1963).

Ibn al-Wardī, ʿUmar b. Muẓaffar: *Dīwān Ibn al-Wardī*, ed. Aḥmad Fawzī al-Hayb (Kuwayt: Dār al-Qalam, 1407/1986).

Kujjah, Hasan & Kujjah, Mohammad: *Ḥalab aš-Šahbāʾ fī ʿuyūn aš-šuʿarāʾ*, 4 vols. (Leiden: Brill, 2022), vol. 1: *Ḥalab fi š-šiʿr al-qadīm: bayna l-qarn as-sābiʿ li-l-milād wa-maṭlaʿ al-qarn al-ʿišrīn*.

Manǧak Bāšā: *Dīwān*, ed. Muḥammad Bāsil ʿUyūn as-Sūd (Dimašq: Manšūrāt al-Hayʾa al-ʿĀmma as-Sūriyya li-l-Kitāb, 2009).

al-Maqqarī, Aḥmad b. Muḥammad: *Nafḥ aṭ-ṭīb min ġuṣn al-Andalus ar-raṭīb wa-ḏikr wazīrihā Lisān ad-Dīn Ibn al-Ḫaṭīb*, ed. Iḥsān ʿAbbās, 8 vols. (Bayrūt: Dār Ṣādir, 1968).

al-Maqrīzī, Aḥmad Ibn ʿAlī: *Al-Mawāʿiẓ wa-l-Iʿtibār fī Ḏikr al-Ḫiṭaṭ wa-l-Āṯār*, 2 vols. (al-Qāhira: Bulāq, 1853).

al-Miṣrī, Muḥammad: *ad-Dīwān ad-Dimašqī: šiʿr nuẓima fī Dimašq qadīman wa-ḥadīṯan* (Bayrūt: Dār al-Fikr al-Muʿāṣira, 1413/1991).

an-Nābulusī, ʿAbd al-Ġanī: *The Arch Rhetorician or the Schemer's Skimmer. A Handbook of Late Arabic badīʿ drawn from ʿAbd al-Ghanī an-Nābulsī's Nafaḥāt al-Azhār ʿalā Nasamāt al-Asḥār*, summarized and systematized by Pierre Cachia (Wiesbaden: Harrassowitz, 1998).

Rabaʿī (ar-), Abū l-Ḥasan: *Faḍāʾil aš-Šām wa-Dimašq*, ed. Ṣalāḥ ad-Dīn al-Munaǧǧid (Dimašq: Maṭbūʿāt al-Maǧmaʿ al-ʿIlmī al-ʿArabī bī-Dimašq, 1950).

as-Suyūṭī, Ǵalāl ad-Dīn: *al-Ḥuǧaǧ al-mubīna fī t-tafḍīl bayna Makka wa l-Madīna*, ed. by ʿAbd Allāh Muḥammad ad-Darwīš (Bayrūt: al-Yamāma, 1405/1985).

as-Suyūṭī, Ǧalāl ad-Dīn: "Sāǧiʿat al-ḥaram fī l-mufāḫara bayn al-Madīna wa-l-Ḥaram", in: *Šarḥ Maqāmāt Ǧalāl ad-Dīn as-Suyūṭī*, ed. Samīr Maḥmūd ad-Durūbī (Bayrūt: Muʾassasat ar-Risāla, 1989), 499–553.

Wakīʿ, Ibn Ḥayyān: *Aḫbār al-quḍāh*, [ed. by ʿAbd al-ʿAzīz Muṣṭafā al-Marāġī], 3 vols. [repr. of Cairo 1366-1369/1947-1950] (Beirut: ʿĀlam al-Kutub, n. d.).

Yāqūt al-Ḥamawī: *Kitāb muʿǧam al-buldān*. 5 vols. (Bayrūt: Dār Ṣādir, 1397/1977).

al-Yunīnī, Quṭb ad-Dīn: *Ḏayl mirʾāt az-zamān*. 4 vols. (Hyderabad: Osmania Oriental Publications Bureau, 1954-1961).

az-Zirindī, ʿAlī b. Yūsuf: *al-Munāẓara bayna Makka wa-l-Madīna*, ed. Saʿīd ʿAbd al-Fattāḥ (al-Qāhira: Dār al-Amīn, 1414/1993).

Secondary Sources

Andrews, Walter G. and Kalpaklı, Mehmet: *The Age of Beloveds: Love and the Beloved in Early-Modern Ottoman and European Culture and Society* (Durham: Duke University Press, 2005).

Antrim, Zayde: "Ibn ʿAsākir's Representations of Syria and Damascus in the Introduction to the Taʾrīkh Madīnat Dimashq", in: *IJMES (International Journal of Middle East Studies)* 38 (2006), 109–129.

Antrim, Zayde: *Routes and Realms: The Power of Place in the Early Islamic World* (New York: Oxford University Press, 2012).

Arazi, Albert: "Matériaux pour l'étude du conflit de préséance entre la Mekke et Medine", in: *Jerusalem Studies in Arabic and Islam* 5 (1984), 177–235.

Bachmann, Peter: "Kairo und Damaskus in Tausendundeiner Nacht", in: *Orte der Literatur*, ed. Werner Frick et al. (Göttingen: Wallstein Verlag, 2003), 50–67.

Bauer, Thomas: "Das Nilzağal des Ibrāhīm al-Miʿmār: Ein Lied zur Feier des Nilschwellenfestes", in: *Alltagsleben und materielle Kultur in der arabischen Sprache und Literatur: Festschrift für Heinz Grotzfeld zum 70. Geburtstag*, ed. Thomas Bauer and Ulrike Stehli-Werbeck (Wiesbaden: Harrassowitz, 2003), 69–88.

Bauer, Thomas: "Dignity at Stake: Mujūn epigrams by Ibn Nubāta (686–768/1287–1366) and his contemporaries", in: *The Rude, the Bad and the Bawdy. Essays in honour of Professor Geert Jan van Gelder*, ed. Adam Talib, Marlé Hammond, Arie Schippers (Cambridge: Gibb Memorial Trust, 2014), 160–185.

Bauer, Thomas: "Ibn Nubātah al-Miṣrī (686–768/1287–1366): Life and Works. Part I: The Life of Ibn Nubātah", in: *Mamlūk Studies Review* 12 (2008), 1–35. – "Part II: The Dīwān of Ibn Nubātah", in: *Mamlūk Studies Review* (2008), 25–69.

Bauer, Thomas: "Ibrāhīm al-Miʿmār: Ein dichtender Handwerker aus Ägyptens Mamlukenzeit", in: *Zeitschrift der Deutschen Morgenländischen Gesellschaft* 152 (2002), 63–93.

Bayyud, Hussein: *Die Stadt in der arabischen Poesie, bis 1258 n. Chr.* (Berlin: Schwarz Verlag, 1988).

Becker, Carl H.: *Islamstudien. Vom Werden und Wesen der islamischen Welt*, 2 vols. (Leipzig: Meyer, 1924/1932).

Bernardini, Michele: "The masnavi-shahrashubs as Town Panegyrics: An International Genre in Islamic Mashriq", in: *Erzählter Raum in Literaturen der islamischen Welt/Narrated Space in the Literature of the Islamic World*, ed. Roxane Haag-Higuchi and Christian Szyska (Wiesbaden: Harrassowitz Verlag, 2001), 81–94.

Bravmann, Meir Max: *The Spiritual Background of Early Islam: Studies in Ancient Arab Concepts* (Leiden: Brill, 2009 [prev. publ. in 1972]).

Bruhns, Hinnerk and Nippel, Wilfried (eds.): *Max Weber und die Stadt im Kulturvergleich* (Göttingen: Vandenhoeck und Ruprecht, 2000).

Bruijn, Peter de (et al.): "S̲h̲ahrangīz", in: *Encyclopaedia of Islam*, Second Edition (Leiden: Brill, 1997), 9: 212.

Burns, Ross. *Damascus. A History* (London: Routledge, 2007).

Cachia, Pierre: "Mawāliyā", in: *Encyclopaedia of Islam*, Second Edition (Leiden: Brill, 1991), 6: 867–868.

Cachia, Pierre: "Mawāliyā", in: *Encyclopedia of Arabic Literature*, ed. Julie Scott Meisami & Paul Starkey (London: Routledge, 1998) 2: 518–519.

Çalış-Kural, Deniz: *Şehrengiz, Urban Rituals and Deviant Sufi Mysticism in Ottoman Istanbul* (London: Ashgate, 2014).

Curtius, Ernst: *Europäische Literatur und lateinisches Mittelalter* (Bern et al.: Francke, 1948).

Degeorge, Gérard: *Damaskus*, 2 vols., [übers. v.] Jürgen Brankel (Wien: Verlag Turia + Kant, 2006).

Elinson, Alexander E: *Looking Back at Al-Andalus. The Poetics of Loss and Nostalgia in Medieval Arabic and Hebrew Literature* (Leiden: Brill, 2015).

Elisséeff, Nikita: "Ḳāsiyūn", in: *Encyclopaedia of Islam*, Second Edition (Leiden: Brill, 1990), 4: 724.

Farès, Bichr: "Mufāk̲h̲ara, 2", in: *Encyclopaedia of Islam*, Second Edition (Leiden Brill, 1993), 7: 309–310.

Gayangos, Pascual de: *The history of the Mohammedan dynasties in Spain.* Extracted from the Nafhu t-tíb min ghosni-l-andalusi-r-rattíb wa táríkh lisánu-d-dín Ibni-l-Khattíb, vol. 1. (London: Oriental Translation Fund, 1840).

Gelder, Geert Jan van: "al-Badrī, Abū l-Tuqā", in: *Encyclopaedia of Islam, Three* [online].

Gelder, Geert Jan van: "City panegyric, in classical Arabic", in: *Encyclopaedia of Islam, Three* [online].

Gelder, Geert Jan van: "Kufa vs Basra: the literary debate", in: *Asiatische Studien* 50 (1996): 339–362.

Gelder, Geert Jan van: "The Conceit of Pen and Sword: On an Arabic Literary Debate", in: *Journal of Semitic Studies* 32 (1987): 329–360.

Giegler, Eugen: *Das Genos der Laudes urbium im lateinischen Mittelalter. Beiträge zur Topik des Städtelobes in der Stadtschilderung.* [Diss. Würzburg 1953].

Gruber, Ernst A: *Verdienst und Rang. Die Faḍā'il als literarisches und gesellschaftliches Problem* (Freiburg i. Br.: Schwarz-Verlag, 1975).

Grunebaum, Gustave E. von: "Aspects of Arabic urban literature, mostly in the ninth and tenth centuries", in: *Islamic Studies* 8 (1969), 281–300.

Grunebaum, Gustave E. von: "Observations on City Panegyrics in Arabic prose", in: *Journal of the American Oriental Society* 64 (1944), 61–65.

Günzel, Stephan: *Topologie. Zur Raumbeschreibung in den Kultur- und Medienwissenschaften* (Bielefeld: transcript, 2007).

Guo, Li: "Reading Adab in Historical Light: Factuality and Ambiguity in Ibn Dāniyāl's 'Occasional Verses' on Mamluk Society and Politics", in: *History and Historiography of Post-Mongol Central Asia and the Mongol East*, ed. Judith Pfeiffer and Sholeh A. Quinn (Wiesbaden: Harrassowitz, 2006), 383–403.

Heidemann, Stefan: "Entwicklung und Selbstverständnis mittelalterlicher Städte in der Islamischen Welt (7.-15. Jahrhundert)", in: *Was machte im Mittelalter zur Stadt? Selbstverständnis, Außensicht und Erscheinungsbilder mittelalterlicher Städte*, ed. by Kurt-Ulrich Jaeschke and Christhard Schrenk (Heilbronn: Stadtarchiv Heilbronn, 2007), 203–244.

Heinrichs, Wolfhart: "Rose versus narcissus: observations on an Arabic literary debate", in: *Dispute poems and Dialogues in the Ancient and Mediaeval Near East: Forms and Types of Literary Debates in Semitic and Related Literatures*, ed. G. J. Reinink and H. L. J. Vanstihout (Leuven: Uitgeverij Peeters, 1991), 179–198.

Hitti, Philip K: *Capital Cities of Arab Islam* (Minneapolis: University of Minnesota Press, 1973).

Hoenerbach, Wilhelm: *Die vulgärarabische Poetik al-Kitāb al-ʿāṭil al-ḥālī wal-muraḫḫaṣ al-ġālī des Ṣafiyyaddīn Ḥillī*, kritisch hrsg. und erklärt von Wilhelm Hoenerbach (Wiesbaden: Steiner, 1956).

Kaplan, Yunus: "Seyrī ve Halep Şehrengizi", in: *Divan Edebiyatı Araştırmalari Dergisi* 14 (2015), 67–92.

Karacasu, Barış: "Türk Edebiyatında Şehrengizler", in: *Türkiye Araştırmaları Literatür Dergisi* 5 (2007), 259–313.

Kaya, Bayram Ali: "Şehrengiz", in: *Diyanet İslam Ansiklopedisi* (Ankara: Türkiye Diyanet Vakfı, 2010), 38: 461–462.

Kugler, Hartmut: *Die Vorstellung der Stadt in der Literatur des Mittelalters* (München: Artemis und Winkler, 1986).

Larkin, Margaret: "Popular poetry in the post-classical period", in: *Arabic Literature in the Post-Classical Period*, ed. Roger Allan and D.

S. Richards (Cambridge: Cambridge University Press, 2006), 191–242.

Lendon, Jon E: *Empire of Honour: The Art of Government in the Roman World* (Oxford: Clarendon Press, 1997).

Masarwa, Alev: "Der Fall Alexandrias in den Städteklagen Ibn Abī Ḥağalahs und seiner Zeitgenossen", in: *The Sultan's Anthologist: Ibn Abī Ḥağala and His Works*, ed. Syrinx von Hees and Nefeli Papoutsakis (Baden-Baden: Ergon, 2017), 307–382.

Masarwa, Alev: "Performing the Occasion: The Chronograms of Māmayya ar-Rūmī (930-985 or 987/1534-1577 or 1579)", in: *The Mamluk-Ottoman Transition: Continuity and Change in Egypt and Bilād aš-Šām in the Sixteenth Century*, ed. by Stephan Conermann and Gül Şen (Bonn: Vandenhoeck & Ruprecht, 2016), 177–206.

Meletinskiĭ, Eleazar Moiseevich: *The Poetics of Myth*, transl. by Guy Lanoue and Alexandre Sadetsky (London: Routledge, 2000).

Menander Rhetor, ed. with translation and commentary by Donald A. Russel and Nigel G. Wilson (Oxford: Clarendon Press, 1981).

Meyer, Carla: *Die Stadt als Thema. Nürnbergs Entdeckung in Texten um 1500* (Ostfildern: Jan Thorbecke Verlag, 2009).

Mundt, Felix: "Der Mensch, das Licht und die Stadt. Rhetorische Theorie und Praxis antiker und humanistischer Stadtbeschreibung", in: *Cityscaping. Constructing and Modelling Images of the City*, ed. Therese Fuhrer, Felix Mundt, Jan Stenger (Berlin / Boston: De Gruyter, 2015), 179–206.

Pellat, Charles: "Marthiya", in: *Encyclopaedia of Islam,* Second Edition, 6: 602–608.

Pernot, Laurent: *Epideictic Rhetoric: Questioning the Stakes of Ancient Praise* (Texas: University of Texas Press, 2015).

Peychev, Stefan: "Max Weber & the Islamic City" [Unpublished paper in: http://www.academia.edu/329856/Max_Weber_and_the_Islamic_City].

Rhoby, Andreas: "Stadtlob und Stadtkritik in der byzantinischen Literatur", in: *Byzantinische Sprachkunst. Studien zur byzantinischen Literatur; gewidmet Wolfram Hörandner zum 65. Geburtstag*, ed. Martin Hinterberger (Berlin: De Gruyter, 2007), 277–295.

Robinson, Cynthia: "'Ubi sunt': Memory and Nostalgia in Taifa Court Culture", in: *Muqarnas* 15 (1998), 20–31.

Rose, Margaret A.: *Parody: Ancient, Modern and Post-modern* (Cambridge: University Press, 2000).

Schluchter, Wolfgang (ed.): *Max Webers Sicht des Islams. Interpretation und Kritik* (Frankfurt a. M.: Suhrkamp, 1987).

Schröder, Stefan: *Zwischen Christentum und Islam: Kulturelle Grenzen in den spätmittelalterlichen Pilgerberichten des Felix Fabri* (Berlin: Akademie Verlag, 2009).

Sinjilawi, Ibrahim: *The Lament for Fallen Cities. A Study of the Development of the Elegiac Genre in Classical Arabic Poetry*. Ph. D. Diss., University of Chicago, 1983.

Šklovskij, Viktor: "Art as Technique", in: *Russian Formalist Criticism: Four Essays*, ed. Lee T. Lemon and Marion J. Reis (Lincoln: Univ. of Nebraska Press, 1965).

Smith, Martyn: "Finding Meaning in the City: al-Maqrīzī's Use of Poetry in the Khiṭaṭ", in: *Mamluk Studies Review* 16 (2012), 143–161.

Snir, Reuven: *Baghdad. The City in Verse* (Cambridge, MA: Harvard University Press, 2013).

Steinschneider, Moritz: *Rangstreit-Literatur: Ein Beitrag zur vergleichenden Literatur- und Kulturgeschichte.* Sitzungsberichte der Kais. Akademie der Wissenschaften in Wien, Philosophisch-historische Klasse (Wien: Verlag Hölder, 1908).

Striedter, Jurij (ed.): *Russischer Formalismus. Texte zur allgemeinen Literaturtheorie und zur Theorie der Prosa* (München: Fink Verlag, 1994).

The Routledge Dictionary of Literary Terms, ed. Peter Child and Roger Fowler (London: Routledge, 2006).

Wagner, Ewald: *Die arabische Rangstreitdichtung und ihre Einordnung in die allgemeine Literaturgeschichte* (Wiesbaden: Steiner Verlag, 1962).

Wagner, Ewald: "Munāẓara", in: *Encyclopaedia of Islam*, Second Edition (Leiden: Brill, 1993), 7: 565–568.

Wagner, Ewald: "Mufākhara, 1", in: *Encyclopaedia of Islam*, Second Edition (Leiden: Brill, 1993), 7: 308–309.

Weber, Max: *Wirtschaft und Gesellschaft: die Stadt* (Tübingen: Mohr (Paul Siebeck), 1922).

Weißhaar-Kiem, Heide: *Lobschriften und Beschreibungen ehemaliger Reichs- und Residenzstädte in Bayern bis 1800: Die Geschichte der Texte und ihre Bibliographie* (Mittenwald: Mäander, 1982).

Wollina, Torsten: "What is a City? Perceptions of Architectural and Social Order in 15th-Century Damascus", in: *ASK Working Paper; 04* (Bonn: Annemarie Schimmel Kolleg - History and Society during the Mamluk Era (1250-1517), 2012).

Zubaida, Sami: "Max Weber's The City and the Islamic City", in: *Max Weber Studies* 6 (2006), 111–118.